THE
MYSTICAL WAY
AND THE
ARTHURIAN QUEST

To John Barman.

THE
MYSTICAL WAY
AND THE
ARTHURIAN QUEST

DEREK BRYCE

First published in 1986   Copyright © Derek Bryce, 1986.
by Llanerch Enterprises,   ISBN 0947992073
Llanerch, Felinfach, Lampeter,
Dyfed, Wales. SA488PJ.

ACKNOWLEDGEMENTS.

The permission of the following owners of copyright is acknowledged with thanks:

Allen and Unwin Ltd. Extracts from **Monkey.** Wu Ch'eng-en. Trans. A Waley. (U.S. copyright: Harper & Row).

Baton Press Ltd. (for Midas Books). Illustration of knight and dragon by Walter Crane (to Spenser's Fairie Queene) from **A History of British Wood Engraving.** A. Garret.

Element Books (for Watkins Publishers). Extracts from **The Hermetic Museum:** A. Lambspring, B. Valentine, The Glory of the World, The Sophic Hydrolith. 1953.

Manchester University Press. Extracts from **Sir Gawain and the Green Knight.** Trans. W. R. J. Barron. 1974.

Thomas Nelson. Illustration of knight on lion from **King Henry V.** W. Shakespeare. 1927.

John Murray Ltd. Extract from **The Monastery of the Jade Mountain.** Peter Goullet. 1961.

Peter Owen. Extract from **The Way and the Mountain.** Marco Pallis. 1960.

Oxford University Press (for Clarendon Press). Extract from **Hermetica.** Trans. Walter Scott. 1924-36.

Penguin Books Ltd. **Don Quixote.** Cervantes. Trans. J. M. Cohen. 1950. Extracts pp. 583 and 939 by permission of Penguin Books Ltd. **A History of the Kings of Britain.** Geoffery of Monmouth. Trans. L. Thorpe. 1966. Extract p. 184 by permission of Penguin Books Ltd.

Routledge and Kegan Paul. Extract from **Of Learned Ignorance.** Nicholas of Cusa. Trans. Fr. G. Heron. 1954.

Triangle (S.P.C.K). Extract from **The Way of a Pilgrim.**

Whitall N. Perry. Extract from W. Law, in **A Treasury of Traditional Wisdom.** George Allen and Unwin. 1971. The work by Whitall N. Perry has been a useful source of reference during the writing of this book.

Thanks are also extended to Mr. R. Rider, Mr. G. Walters, and staff of the library at St Davids University College, Lampeter, Mr R. Brinkley of the Library at University College, Aberystwyth, and Mrs N. Jenkins and staff at the National Library of Wales, for help with literature and incunabula; also Miss Pia de Richmont of the Catholic Truth Society, for information; Mr Paul Larkin and the Chertsey Museum for illustrations of Chertsey tiles; Mr David Lewis for illustrations; and all friends, past and present, whose conversations have contributed to this book.

CONTENTS

LIST OF ILLUSTRATIONS.

*Designs from tiles from Chertsey Abbey, courtesy Chertsey Museum. The Benedictine abbey at Chertsey existed from the seventh century, until its dissolution in 1537. The decorated floor tiles have been said to be the finest mediaeval tiles to have been produced in Britain. They were made in the abbey in the 13th century, and the circular designs are approximately nine inches in diameter. They were collected during the second half of the 19th century by Dr Mainwaring Shurlock, who produced a large book containing facsimilies of the tiles, entitled 'Tiles from Chertsey Abbey,' in 1885.

PREFACE.

This book started off with the title of 'The Meaning of the Quest.' It was intended to be an explanation of the symbolism and profound meaning of the knightly quest. It soon became clear, however, that the meaning could not be adequately explained within the context of the Arthurian Saga alone. It could only be fully understood by taking into account the world-view of ancient and traditional times, and the language and methods of the mystical ways of those times. The title was therefore changed to 'The Mystical Way and the Arthurian Quest.'

The first few chapters have therefore been devoted to the mystical way in general, to familiarize the reader with the ancient and traditional world-view, and with the variety of ways and methods of the mystery cults and religions. These first chapters have been aimed at providing a fabric within which the profound meaning of the Arthurian tales can be explained, in the middle section of the book. The latter includes not only the story of the Holy Grail, but also the love-quest, as typified by the romance of Tristan and Isoude, the quest of the princess, and the story of Sir Gawain and the Green Knight. The final chapter of the book deals with the form taken by the quest after the Middle Ages; it ends with a discussion of its relevance to modern times.

References to the literature have been given wherever possible, but in some cases no references are given because the source is from oral tradition; this is true also for some of the quotations from Islam, which exists both as a written and an oral tradition, and many of the quotations in this book have been translated verbally by Arabic-speaking friends and former students.

'There is nothing new under the sun,' and of course none of the ideas in this book are 'new;' they have been collected by reading widely and from conversations with many people. The reader may, however, find something new in this book in the way in which it brings together many ideas, sayings, and facts which have hitherto been scattered, and forms a context within which the meaning of the quest may be better understood.

Derek Bryce
Wales, 1986.

2. The Knight
(from early edition of Chaucer)

CHAPTER 1. THE QUEST.

Although the theme of the quest is world-wide, including the famous story of Jason and the Golden fleece, and the alchemical quest of the Philosopher's Stone, quest stories form an outstanding feature of the Celtic Tradition. Sometimes the object of the quest is a talisman described as having wonderful or magical properties, or a most sacred object such as the Holy Grail; sometimes it is a golden-haired princess in need of rescue from a wicked magician, or a king who has been imprisoned in a dungeon by a usurping tyrant; sometimes it is a lost sister; sometimes it is a handsome prince being sought after by his beloved. Many of the Celtic quest tales, especially the Arthurian ones, concern members of a warrior, or knightly caste, but there are others where the hero is an artisan, tradesman, or peasant-farmer, and some which centre around a heroine. Many quest tales belong to the class of truly great, or inspired literature which is characterized by a deeper variety of meanings hidden behind the literal one. The profound interpretation of such tales is of the human soul in search of the Spirit. Most of these tales feature a hero who represents the human soul in an active state of seeking; a few tales feature a heroine who represents the human soul in a state of passivity when face-to-face with the divine.

The aim of this book is to show how the theme of spiritual development and realization is hidden within stories of the quest; how the quest symbolises a spiritual journey. In order to understand this, it is necessary to look into the mystical and esoteric, or hidden ways of the ancient and traditional worlds, both East and West. The next four chapters are therefore devoted to the latter, because the Arthurian quest can only be properly explained and understood within this framework.

CHAPTER 2. EAST AND WEST, ANCIENT AND MODERN.

The gulf between the attitudes, beliefs, and philosophical outlook of the modern West and the traditional East only came with the Renaissance; it widened steadily in Post-Renaisance times, and culminated in the peculiar situation we have today where most of the East is actively and willingly westernizing itself and abandoning its traditions, whilst some westerners are actively seeking a return to similar mystical and traditional ways.

If we go back to the Middle Ages and before, although there were differences in culture and language, the gulf referred to above did not exist. If at times there were instances of opposition between cultures, the crusades for example, there was at least understanding between an intellectual elite.

Although most people see their own religion as the only true one, some of the more esoteric, or mystical religious writers have understood the transcendent unity behind all religions.

Christ's "no man cometh to the Father but by me" (John XIV, 6) is generally interpreted by Christians as invalidating other religions; the esoteric explanation is that here it is the Logos, the Word, speaking through Christ. In other words, no Christian can come to the Father except by Christ; no man can come to God except by the Logos*. Likewise, "other sheep have I, which are not of this fold" (John X, 16) can be interpreted historically as a reference to Christianity spreading amongst the Gentiles, and also, as the Logos speaking, as a reference to other religions. Christ's "in my Father's house are many mansions" (John XIV, 2) can also be interpreted as a cryptic reference to other religions and traditions. Some Christians have recognized the validity of other religions, or the spiritual greatness of their Pagan ancestors. St Justin, one of the Church Fathers, said: "All such as lived according to the divine word in them, which was in all men, were Christians, such as Socrates and Heraclitus, and

---

*Matgioi points out that in Chinese we find almost the same word; the ideogram for the universal and invisible dragon, representing the Word, is transcribed as 'long,' pronounced with the 'o' long and the 'n' almost silent; in the old vice-kingdoms of central China it is pronounced without any 'n' at all!

others among the Greeks." The twelfth century scholastic philosopher, Bernard of Chartres, compared the ancients, both Christian and pre-Christian, with Giants. He used to say we are like dwarfs sitting on the shoulders of Giants. He would add that we can see further than the ancients, not because of any special abilities of our own, but because they raised us so high. Dante, who had to contend with the Roman Church of his times, dare not risk giving spiritual status to Virgil, his first guide. He had to content himself by declaring that he (Dante) was the greatest poet since Virgil, thereby implying the latter's spiritual eminence. Dante did, however, manage to put one of his Pagan predecessors, Trajan, in Heaven by using the literary device of of having him miraculously resurrected through the prayers of Pope Gregory the Great, converted, dead a second time, and saved. Those with the requisite understanding could see from this that Dante recognized spirituality in the pre-Christian Classical Tradition. Early this century, a Spanish writer, Asin Palacios, pointed out that there are striking parallels between the works of Dante and those of Islamic writers such as Ibn 'Arabi and Abu 'Ala al-Ma'arri. Since then, a number of commentators have recognized the great debt owed by Dante's work to Islam*. Dante seems to have been associated with a tertiary order of Templars known as *La Fede Santa;* he was also a member of a mystical and initiatic secret society called the *fedilio d'amore*, which possibly had links with the East and the Templars. His link with Islam was probably via the Templars. Dante placed a character named Macometto amongst the sowers of discord in Hell. Some Italian commentators have transcribed this name as Maometto, some English as Mahomet, implying the Prophet of Islam. There can be little doubt that Dante knew the correct pronunciation of the name of Muhammad, and he deliberately mis-spelt it in order to satisfy the Roman Church and many of his readers on the one hand, and his own conscience on the other. The misspelling made Macometto a fictitious character for Dante and those of his readers who understood the transcendent unity of religions. Along with Macometto, Dante also included Ali, the cousin and son-in-law of the Prophet. In this case, Dante spelt the name correctly. The succession

*See the book by William Anderson.

of Ali to the Caliphate caused the Shi'ite schizm in Islam, and this may be why Dante saw him in a bad light. Most Muslims, needless to say, would not agree with him on this point, for the schizm occurred after Ali's death, and not during his lifetime.

Papal comments on the validity of other religions have been rare; Pius XI, however, when addressing his Apostolic Delegate to Libya, is reported as saying: "Do not think you are going among infidels. Muslims attain to salvation. The ways of providence are infinite."

Like most Christians, the majority of Muslims see their religion as the only true one; and this despite two passages in the Koran: "And we have sent prophets to other nations, some of whom you know, and some of whom you do not know"... and "As for the people of the book, providing they believe and do good works, they shall have nothing to fear." The phrase 'people of the book' refers to those that have a revealed book or scripture, the Jews and the Christians. One of the most esoteric of Islamic writers, Ibn 'Arabi, the famous twelfth century Spanish mystic, wrote: "My heart is the q'aaba of the faithful, the cloister of the monk, and the temple of the idol worshipper." The saying of Muhammad to the effect that "he who sees me, or hears of me, and does not follow, is lost," must be interpreted in its historical and geographical context, for God does not contradict himself. It may be interpreted as referring to those who do not have a valid religion, and who, on hearing of Muhammad, do not follow. At that time, the old Arabian religion was becoming invalid through senility, and many of the newer Christian sects flourishing there were likewise invalid through having become heretical. The saying was therefore literally true for the Arabian Peninsula at that time. The Islamic concept of a merciful God would likewise be contradicted by the idea of only one valid religion, with reference to the pre-Columbian peoples of the New World who were without any contact with the religions of the Old World. This last comment also applies to those Christians who see their religion as the only true one.

Some readers may pose the question that if the transcendent unity of religions is true, why is it not made clearer in the Divine Revelations? The answer is that each revelation must take into account the general mentality of the people to whom it is addressed. If the revelation had been more open on this point, many Christians of limited understanding would have reasoned that since Muslims attained Salvation, and could have more than one wife and concubines, so could they; many Muslims, similarly, would have reasoned that since Christians attained salvation, and they could drink alcohol and eat pork, so could they; each one forgetting that their particular revelation was designed to suit the needs of their own mentality and make-up. Each path has its own characteristics. To cross the desert one wears sandals and takes a camel; to cross the arctic one wears snow shoes and uses huskies or reindeer. To attempt to mix elements from different religions could be like wearing sandals in the arctic, or snow shoes in the desert. In modern times one can, of course, learn a great deal from other religions, and gain a great deal of support from them. What is implied here relates to practice; one can only travel on one path at a time, but one may learn much from those who have travelled on others.

Further evidence of understanding between traditions can be seen, for example, in one of the synagogues in Toledo, which is architecturally Islamic and has an internal frieze of scallop shells, the symbol of St James, the patron saint of Spain. In other words, the Jews in Toledo had their synagogue designed and built in Islamic style, and decorated with a Christian motif. Similarly, outside the walls of Segovia in Spain, there is a Templar church which has (or had) a painting hanging on the wall, of a Muslim in the act of making invocatory prayer. Spain in the Middle Ages was a meeting point of three cultures; its proximity to North Africa also made it a natural link between East and West, a link which was only broken by the expulsion of the Muslims, begun in 1492.

What has come down to us of ancient Megalithic and Celtic art and music has more in common with oriental, than it has with modern western art and music. We once knew an Indian who, on hearing a record of an old Irish air, said "but that's Indian music!" Without developing this theme further - which could easily fill a book its own right - we simply wish to point out that prior to the Renaissance, although cultural groups may have appeared different or even opposed, they contained many equivalents, and there was more understanding between them than has often been thought.

In the ancient world, the far-western Celtic region seems to have been held in high regard. The oldest possible references to this are to be found in the ancient Daoist writings of China. In the book of Lie Zi (Lieh Tzu) we read of Emperor Mu's wanderings:

"It was then that, with his eight famous horses each of a different hue, he undertook his famous expedition beyond the western frontiers. He was accompanied by Zoa Fu who drove his chariot, Qu He who served as groom, and Shen Bai who drove the wagon assisted by Ben Rong. After having covered a thousand stages, he reached the Ju Sou tribe, who gave him swans' blood to drink and washed his feet with koumiss (two fortifiers). The following night was spent on the banks of the Red Torrent. The next day the emperor climbed Mount Kun Lun, visted the Yellow Emperor's ancient palace, and built a cairn in memory of his visit. Next he visited Xi Wang Mu, and was entertained by her near the Green Lake. They exchanged toasts and the emperor did not hide the fact that it was painful for him to have to go back. After having contemplated the place where the sun sets at the end of its diurnal course of ten thousand stages, he made his way back to the empire."

The book of Lie Zi dates from the second century B.C. and the traditional dates for the reign of Emperor Mu are 1001 to 947 B.C. Elsewhere in the Daoist writings we find brief references to ancient voyages "across the western ocean" to a highly-esteemed "far-distant island" described in one instance as the land of the "Four Masters." Lao Zi (Lao Tzu) the Old Master of the Daoist Tradition is, according to legend, said to have become weary of the decadent state of the Chinese Empire (around 500 B.C.) and to have ended his life in the Far West.

One is left wondering if the "western ocean" quoted above refers to the Mediterranean, if the "Four Masters" refers to the kings of Ireland, and if "Xi Wang Mu" is not the Lady of the Lake who, in the Celtic Tradition is a fay, a psychic being gifted with great longevity. There is, of course, virtually no historical evidence to corroborate any of this, and some historians, such as Wieger, have placed Emperor Mu's travels in the region of the Pamir.

The Pamir is a dissected plateau where the Himalayan, Kunlun and Tienshan mountains meet. The Kunlun mountains run from the Pamir along the northern border of Tibet. On the face of it, this would seem to oppose a far-western interpretation of Emperor Mu's travels. However, when ethnic groups travel, they tend to take their place-names with them. For example there is a Lango in North Norway, and one in Lancashire, England; there are Black Mountains in the south of Wales, and in the south of Brittany. Although Emperor Mu's travels were perhaps in the region of Tibet, there remains the possibility that there may have been more than one Kun Lun mountain(s). We are not trying to 'prove a point' on this question, but think it is worth keeping an open mind about it. One fragment of supporting evidence can be seen in the discovery of jade axe heads in the Megalithic tumulus of Mané-er-H'oeck, in Brittany. Rolleston, commenting on this find, stated that "jade is not found in the native state in Europe, nor nearer than China." Whilst these axe heads could have reached Brittany through intermediaries, there still remains the possibility of a direct connection. A few other concordances can be seen in the special significance of the dragon to both the Celts and the Chinese, and their prediliction for triads. (The Chinese seem also to have a preference for round tables!)

If there is any truth in this idea that the Far West was regarded as spiritually important in the ancient world, it would lend support to the Glastonbury Legends. The latter, immortalized by William Blake's hymn "Jerusalem" imply that Christ spent his "lost years" in Britain. The legends further claim that Joseph of Arimathea came to Glastonbury; some say that he founded the first Christian Church there, in 63 A.D., others that he brought with him the Holy Grail, the vessel containing the blood of Christ. The Glastonbury Legends did not appear in written form until near the end of the Middle Ages. There are those who believe they were fabricated in the thirteenth century; but there are others who believe they may have been based on oral traditions coming down from more ancient times. Whatever the truth, it is a fact that the early Celtic Church differed from the Roman Church, notably in its monastic organization, the way the monks shaved their heads, and in the date for celebrating Easter. These differences imply an early and 'independent' origin

15

for the Celtic Church. It would seem that it flourished for a time alongside Druidism, and some of the older Celtic Christian legends show respect for the Druids.

Whatever the truth of the foregoing, it is a fact that much of the ancient knowledge had been lost from mainland Europe by the time Charlemagne established peace in the West. The ancient writings had, however, been preserved by the Irish Celts, and Scotus Erigina took them with him when, in the mid-ninth century, he went over from Ireland to the court of Charles the Bold.

Having indicated that in ancient times the West was not so markedly different from the East, and was perhaps even highly esteemed by ancient Orientals, we can say that the question is not so much one of East and West as of ancient and modern. Traditional civilizations take the view that existence is made up of three worlds: spiritual, psychic, and corporeal. The separation of the upper, from the lower waters in Genesis represents the separation of the spiritual from the psychic. In the ancient world, the concept of 'matter' or 'material' applied to both the psychic world and the corporeal, hence the concept of a psychic 'body' as well as a corporeal one. Sometimes the corporeal state was regarded simply as a modality of the world of the psyche, like a 'condensation' of it. In the old days, the person was also regarded as superior to the individual.

People brought up and educated in modern times can easily become confused when considering ancient and traditional cultures. This is because they have been brought up with a different world-view, influenced by Cartesian dualism. The modern dualistic world-view of 'mind and matter,' 'body and soul,' has changed the concept of matter, restricting it to the corporeal state alone; it has confounded the spiritual with the psychic; and in its most extreme form it tends to regard things of the mind or soul as consequences of material complexity, such as a complex nervous system, which is an inversion of the spirit-psyche-body hierarchy of the ancient world-view. In modern English the concept of the person has become inferior to that of the individual, as is witnessed by the butler saying: "Madam, there is a lady at the door"..... "Madam, there is a person at the door." Likewise in modern English the personality has tended to become confused with the individuality, or regarded as an aspect of it. These

16

changes in world-view, and the meanings of words, must always be kept in mind when reading Pre-Renaissance and traditional writings.

ʍ themselves each as fulfil-
as no strong cult of the in-
ιe modern world. A conse-
ιcient works of art, and lit-
mous, but this does not mean
ɔy great masters. This holds
ιch are far from being the
ality of the people. On top
st ancient traditional peoples
; a chronology of events, ac-
ɣ had of history was in the
ıf interest as stories having a
ιore than anything else. In a
ed as historical events which
aken out of time. Their time-
:s them applicable to other
ɔces.

ntal difference in outlook be-
:rn worlds, concerns time and
race. The great spiritual tra-
the human race as a race in
aecune. ... ιn doctrine of the fall implies
that humanity has lost something it once had. The Prophet Muhammad said: "After me there will not come a time which is not worse than the preceding one." Shakespeare, in King John (IV, i) causes Arthur of Brittany to say, as he is about to be blinded: "Ah, none but in this iron age would do it," implying that only in this later, base age would man stoop to such vile acts. The Hindus have a highly developed cosmological theory which describes humanity as passing through great cycles, or manvantaras, of 60,000 years. Each manvantara is divided into four lesser cycles, or yugas, in the proportion of 4:3:2:1, so that the last yuga is of 6000 years. The passage from one yuga to the next is marked by drastic events followed by a degree of spiritual redress which is adapted to the conditions of the new yuga. At the end of the manvantara there is a phase of destruction followed by a new humanity returned to its primordial state. The four yugas of the Hindus correspond with the ancient western notion of the ages of gold, silver, bronze (or brass), and iron. The

17

Biblical Flood probably marks, for the Semitic races, the passage from one such age to the next; Noah's prophetic function being to guard the tradition and transmit it in a form adapted to the new age. According to the Hindu Tradition, we are now approaching the end of the Age of Kali. It is not, however, possible to put a precise date on the end of this age, because we do not have an exact date for its beginning; furthermore, the passage from one age to the next may not be instantaneous and marked by a single event; it could equally be marked by a series of events over a period of years.

The modern notion of progress stands in sharp contrast to the above views. Although it can be traced back to the French Revolution, and Lamark, the theory of indefinite human progress is largely due to Herbert Spencer. Many people erroneously impute this theory to Darwin, but he was concerned with theories of the origin of biological species, and he deliberately excluded Spencer's theory from his own. Spencerian progressivism only found its way into biological evolutionary writings after Darwin, since when it has exerted a very strong influence on the modern mentality. Only in very recent times, under the current threats of nuclear disaster, 'peaceful' or warlike, chemical and biological warfare, environmental deterioration, and world population increase, has the theory weakened a little.

We said above that the fundamental difference between the ancient and modern view of time and humanity may be only apparent, and this is why: The traditional view takes man's spiritual state as its starting point, regarding this as of prime importance. The modern view of progress, whatever were the personal views of Herbert Spencer, takes materialism as its starting point, with only a sentimental approach to moral, and other values. It owes its success to the indisputable technological progress of the nineteenth and twentieth centuries. Looked at this way, the two theories are not in conflict; they only come into conflict when the theory of progress is regarded as indefinite and extended from materialism to spirituality. What little we know of human civilizations shows them having a legendary beginning, with heroes, saints, and sages, a phase of flowering, often with the development of architecture and the traditional arts and sciences, followed by a decline and ending. Often the period of decline is associated with the production of spectacular artefacts. This would, of course, correspond with a cyclic view. Time alone will tell whether the present-day technological progress will lead to the Utopia which has so long been promised 'just around the corner,' or to an end in a phase of destruction which so many now fear.

Whatever the views of the reader on the foregoing, it is important to bear these differences in world-view in mind, whenever any aspects of the ancient and traditional worlds are being considered. One important point to note is that man seems to produce spectacular results whichever way he turns himself. Modern man, turned 'outwards' and 'downwards,' towards materialism, has produced the impressive developments we see today, in transport, communications, mechanisation, and all the rest. Men at other times, turned 'inwards' and 'upwards,' towards spirituality rather than materialism, may have produced spectacular results of another kind. We often tend to be sceptical about tales from other times which are beyond our own experiences; perhaps people from those other times would have found tales of this civilization hard to believe. To illustrate this last point there is a story, told by the American painter George Catlin, of the Assiniboin Chief Wu ju jon, who, in the early 1830's, was the first of his tribe to visit Washington. Chief Wu ju jon returned to his tribe and told them of the wonders of the white man's world that he had seen there, but they refused to believe him and branded him the biggest liar the world had ever seen. He died soon after, in disrepute.

One of the problems of modern times is that man, turned materialist, is too big for this world. His abilities in material terms are so great that he runs the risk of exhausting and destroying one natural environment after another, and, if it were possible, even one planet after another, just like a child who plays with its toys and breaks them. The old civilizations were based on a hierarchy in which the spiritual was seen as superior to the material, and material things and technology were only of secondary importance, to provide a basic sustenance. The old civilizations generally aimed at living in harmony with the environment, or at least in not depleting it of its resources; only in the late, degenerate phases of some old civilizations do we see evidence of environmental deterioration, from over-grazing, for example.

19

This is not meant to imply that one should oppose technology, and it would be foolish not to take advantage of the material compensations of these times. Zhuang Zi (Chuang Tzu), the second century B.C. Daoist Sage, saw inventions in a bad light, not because they were 'bad' in themselves, but because they led man away from the spiritual life; he nevertheless added that now the Chinese had invented a counterbalanced device for irrigating crops, it would be foolish for anyone to return to lugging buckets of water. The materialism of our times is the way of this world; wishing to oppose it would be like wishing the incoming tide to turn back on the seashore. The dangers of anti-materialism are that instead of returning man to spirituality, it may have no other result than to lead him into the labyrinth of a drug-and-fantasy world. What is important is to see that materialism cannot satisfy man's spiritual needs. Those who see this, should seek the spiritual life and leave the world to go its way; becoming preoccupied with criticism will not lead to a spiritual way. Man's needs are spiritual, psychic, and material*; the problem with a materialistic world is that it attempts to satisfy all needs by offering more and more of the same thing. It is no use offering more and more food to someone with a raging thirst; likewise offering more and more material possessions to someone with spiritual longing, will not satisfy that longing.

*Man's basic material needs are food, clothing, housing and warmth; his psychic, or psychological needs are to have satisfactory relations with family, friends, acquaintances, colleagues, and others; his spiritual needs concern the meaning of life, to give it a sense of purpose.

CHAPTER 3. DIVERSE WAYS; UNDERLYING UNITY.

In most traditional civilizations and cultures, one can distinguish two ways, corresponding with two different types of person.

Exoterism, or the outer way, is the one followed by the majority. It consists in following a set of legal and moral rules relating to individual behaviour and social organisation, and in the accomplishment of prescribed rites, or partaking of them. The exoteric way is presented as a guide for people to follow so that they shall have nothing to fear after death. In the western revealed religions this takes the form of a covenant between God and man, whereas, for example in Confucianism, the Chinese exoterism, it appears more like a set of rules derived by human reasoning, albeit from superior principles. Those who follow an exoteric way must await death and the beyond before they may have any possibility of spiritual realisation or transformation; the oriental traditions often regard such people as trapped in the endless chain of births and deaths. Generally speaking, the ultimate concept of exoterism does not go beyond the oneness of being, God, although in the case of Buddhism the concept is of the state of being, rather than being itself (a non-theistic perspective, sometimes wrongly called atheistic).

Esoterism, or the inner way, consists in living a spiritual life with the possibility of realisation or transformation even before bodliy death. This way remains hidden:

"I have meat to eat that you know not of."
(St John IV, 32).
"There are more things in heaven and earth, Horatio, than are dreamed of in your philosophy."
(Shakespeare, Hamlet IV).

Esoteric knowledge has, until very recent times, generally been kept secret, not in order to prevent the masses having access to it, but because they simply could not understand it and could risk misusing it or becoming confused:

"Do not cast pearls before swine."
(St Matthew VII, 6).

The fact that many things which have been kept secret in

the past are nowadays made public, is one of the compensations for living in these times; it has its risks, but it is necessary because of the decay of many of the old secret societies, and the destruction of the craft initiations by the Industrial Revolution. The ultimate esoteric concept goes beyond the oneness of being, to beyond-being, the Absolute, Dao (the Principle) of Chinese esoterism, represented in the western religions of Semitic origin as the Most High God.

We have pointed out in the last chapter that legendary sources imply that the Far West may have been *the* place for seeking esoteric spiritual knowledge in ancient times. Classical writers such as Pomponius Mela give us to understand that the Druids did not commit their teaching to writing, and kept their oral tradition secret from the people, restricting it to themselves and their disciples. To have some idea of esoterism in the times of the Druids we must first look at it elsewhere; we shall see later how some of our observations may be used for interpreting the myths and legends which have come down to us from the ancient Western Tradition.

In esoterism, the Hindus distinguish three ways of yoga, corresponding with three different types of person: A way of knowledge (jnana-yoga), a way of love (bhakti-yoga), and a way of action (karma-yoga). There are, of course, other types of yoga. The three referred to above represent three basic ways; other types of yoga, such as hatha-yoga, the yoga of breathing exercises, refer more to method than to a basic way. These three basic ways do not mean, for example, that someone following a way of love does not have knowledge and never acts; it simply means that the element of love and devotion is central and paramount for the person in question. Christianity started off as an esoteric religion; the early Christians used not the cross, but the fish as their symbol, representing the guide across the 'lower waters' of Genesis, the world of the psyche. They were esoteric by virtue of their maintaining a state of near-continual internal prayer. When Christianity became the official religion of the Roman Empire, it in a sense made a sacrifice, becoming exoteric in order to cater for a larger mass of people incapable of following the esoteric way. This change is made clear in the ceremony for the ordination of a Roman Catholic priest, which speaks of the admittance of lesser men: "...to the High Priests first chosen by Thee... Thou didst give men of less degree* and of subordinate rank as their associates and helpers" (pre-Vatican II ceremony). The same ceremony, however, also contains an esoteric reference, to Melchisedec, who, in the Old Testament, was Priest of the Most High God. The early Celtic Church seems to have been esoteric, and the lives of some of the old Celtic saints are highly mystical in character. In the Middle Ages, the Christian monasteries provided esoteric possibilities for certain types of person, although not all monks were so inclined. Contemplative, devotional, and active monastic orders corresponded in theory with the Hindu ways of knowledge, love, and action. We should add, however, that true intellectuals - the Sage-hermits so often met with in the old Celtic legends - have been less common in historical times in the West. Thomas Aquinas stands out in this category from the Middle Ages; and the Templars were no doubt a repository of ancient and eso-teric knowledge, as well as forming a link between East and West. Most Christian contemplatives have, in fact, followed more a way of love, than of knowledge, for there is no hard and fast dividing line between the three cat-egories. Monasticism apart, in Mediaeval Europe, there were ways of action - orders of knighthood for nobles - craft initiations for plebeians - and the traditional sci-ences such as alchemy. There were also secret societies, one of which we have mentioned in connection with Dante.

In Mediaeval Spain, Islam flourished for seven centuries alongside Christianity. Islam differs fundamentally from Christianity, in not having a priesthood, all Muslims being, in a sense, their own priest and able to perform their own rites. The use, by the modern press, of the term Islamic clergy, refers to religious notables; they are not priests in the sense of performing rites which they alone can ac-complish. Ibn 'Arabi, the great Spanish Islamic mystic, wrote of three categories of the 'men of God:' Devotees, Sufis, and the People of Blame. Devotees he described as being exactly what their name implies, and being on the

*Where St Paul writes that all Christians are 'holy' or 'saints,' he is ad-dressing himself to his esoteric contemporary Christians, and not those of the future exoterism. Many modern fundamentalist Christians assume that everything in the Pauline letters is addressed to them, thereby deluding themselves and denaturing the terms 'holy' and 'saint.'

indistinct border between exoterism and esoterism. The Sufis may be described as esoteric Muslims; they cannot, however, be compared directly with Christian monks, for monasticism is forbidden in Islam and each sufi disciple has to earn his living in the world, and generally marries and raises a family. Ibn 'Arabi described his third group, the People of Blame, or *Malamatiyyah*, with the highest esteem of all; they are people of high spiritual state who live hidden in society, acting generally just like all the others. They are called the People of Blame because their actions, based on superior knowledge or intuition, sometimes seem strange to others, who criticise and blame them because they do not know their interior motives. Sometimes they deliberately behave so as to incur scorn, as a means of hiding their spiritual rank from the people. Shaikh Darqawi, who was a Sufi, would sometimes behave in this way, for example by going out wearing three hats; this example also shows us that there is not always a clear dividing line between the Sufis and the People of Blame.

Ibn 'Arabi's reference to the People of Blame often living hidden amongst the people, thus leads us to another esoteric category; the hidden Sage. The Daoist writings of China also contain references to hidden Sages, and there is little doubt that such types have existed everywhere. They account for the existence of masterpieces of profound folk-literature and the like, which, as we have already said, are not simply the products of the 'people.'

We must also mention the way of the Shaman, for Shamanism figures in many of the western quest tales. The Shamanistic Tradition has its origins among the tribes living around the Arctic Circle. After the last Ice Age, these tribes must have been living further south, and then migrated northwards after the retreating ice. They did not all migrate back at the same time; the Yakuts, for instance, seem to have moved back to Siberia comparatively recently, taking with them the knowledge of iron tools, yet having retained their Shamanism all the time. Shamanism seems to have been left behind in the West so that it later became a part of the old Celtic religion. It seems to have persisted into the early Christian period, and some early Celtic Christians, to whom legend attributes shamanistic powers, may have been Shaman-Druids who had been converted to Christianity.

24

Shamanism takes a pantheistic view, seeing everything in God, and God in everything. When a Shaman takes on the form of an animal, he is, in a sense, experiencing God in the creation. A Shaman who successively experiences one kind of animal transformation after another, can be said to be on an esoteric pathway, experiencing the different spiritual states which each represent, with the ultimate aim of transcending them all. Some Shamans stop short at a single animal transformation; they then begin to use the animal power they have acquired for personal motives, for example, to overcome another Shaman; they can be said to have become distracted from the esoteric way into the occult, which can lead to sorcery.

Apart from experiencing animal transformations, many Shamans also travelled in the other world, the world of the psyche, either during drug-induced states of trance, or simply during sleep. In some traditions where Shamanism is still practised, it is forbidden to wake a sleeping Shaman. The reason given for this is that his soul may be absent, and waking his body may prevent its return, leaving a body without a soul, which may become possessed and turn into a monstrous being*. In the early days of Celtic Christianity, many Druids must have been converted and introduced elements of Paganism, including the practice of Shamanism, into the new religion where they survived briefly. Rolleston, for example, points out that so many Christian monasteries sprung up so rapidly after the conversion of Ireland by St Patrick, as to imply the wholesale conversion of Druidic Colleges. Some evidence of shamanistic practices of the soul leaving the body and travelling may be seen in episodes of many of the knightly quest tales, where the knight crosses a boundary, often marked by an expanse of water, a forest, or a desert**, and has an adventure in the 'other world.'

The frequent reference to hermit-Shamans in many of the old Celtic legends indicates that many Druids practised Shamanism. Many of the old legends also refer to magical practices, and we must conclude that they also practised Traditional Magic. The Druids, however, seem to have been the guardians of a great deal of esoteric knowledge, and we must express the opinion that they

*See Luzel's Celtic Folk-Tales.
**A desert implies a wilderness in the old stories.

practised Shamanism and Magic more as accessories, as applied traditional sciences, than as their central theme.

The question may be asked: 'Why so many different ways in esoterism?' The Hindus distinguish the three basic ways we have mentioned, but Ibn 'Arabi said that in a sense there are as many different ways as people. One reason for this concerns language. The 'gift of tongues' received by the disciples of Christ can be interpreted as a miraculous ability to speak foreign languages, or a gift of the 'key' to foreign languages, which makes their learning easy. The two interpretations above are the literal ones; the profound explanation is an ability to speak to each person in a language he or she can understand. For example, one can speak in English to a surgeon about a pneumosectomy, but to a non-medical person one may have to speak of a lobe of a lung being removed. This is a crude example, for in esoterism the language cannot be direct - hence the Gospels' 'he spoke to them in parables so that those who had ears to hear, could hear...' - and as the language has to be indirect, it must be appropriate to the listener's habitual way of thinking.

There is an old western saying: 'When you're alone, if you're not with God, you're with the Devil.' Similarly, the Islamic Tradition recognises two states of being - dhikr-Llah, or 'remembrance' of God - and ghaflah, or 'forgetfulness.' On any way, exoteric or esoteric, there is a constant tendency to fall into forgetfulness; to become distracted. In the ancient world, every craft, institution, and human activity had its own special language which was at one and the same time practical and profoundly symbolic. Every human activity was thus accompanied by frequent symbolic 'reminders' of a profound nature. The practice of a trade, craft, or almost any other human activity involved the participant in a language he or she could understand, and which, because of its profound symbolism, could function as an esoteric language for those capable of understanding it.

The Prophet Muhammad, on returning from a warlike expedition, said: "We are returning from the lesser holy war, to the great holy war," meaning the war one has to fight within oneself. This symbolic language of holy warfare is not restricted to Islam. It is, moreover, a language that could be understood by a member of a warrior, or knightly class. Such a knight or warrior could easily understand tales of heroic adventures, and battles undertaken out of devotion to a beautiful lady, or tales of the heroic rescue of a beautiful princess from the clutches of an evil magician. He could easily transpose such stories to ones of devotion to the Blessed Virgin, or, in pre-Christian times, a Goddess. He could also understand them as referring to the Spirit within, and a holy war against the evil of his own self. The same knight, or warrior, would no doubt be bored to tears by a discourse on the same spiritual theme, couched in the language of scholars, their manner of speaking being inappropriate to his way of thinking.

The practical languages of traditional crafts were often highly symbolic, including macrocosmic symbolism, referring to the universe, and microcosmic, referring to man's spiritual becoming. The ancient practising stonemason was working with a familiar symbolism which represented a complete cosmological symbolism derived from the idea of the Great Arthitect of the Universe. The traditional boat builder, each time he built a boat, used a constructional language which reminded him of the spiritual nature of the human microcosm. The weaver's craft was symbolic of creation, destiny, and becoming... Many more examples could, of course, be given, but the few above should suffice to indicate that each craft had a language capable of esoteric transposition so that each practitioner who was capable of understanding, had access to profound esoteric knowledge in his or her own specialist language. We shall give a detailed example in a later chapter. It should go without saying that not all craftsmen in the ancient world achieved the spiritual ideals of their craft... Just as there were orders of knighthood, so crafts were often organised into guilds which had their own initiation ceremonies and rituals. The ancient craft organisations were primarily concerned with spiritual realisation; the welfare and material protection of their members was an important, but secondary consideration; in this, they were markedly different from modern trade unions.

Traditional sciences such as alchemy, represent another esoteric way having its own special language. The true alchemists were not greedy for gold in the literal sense. For them, the transmutation of base metals into gold symbolised the spiritual transformation of the base human being. Their alchemical science was a source of a rich symbolic language, with terms such as crystallisation, pre-cipitation, solution, dissolution, sublimation, all referring to a spiritually transformist way. The true alchemy was accomplished within their own interior; in so far as they practised it externally, it was primarily with a view to reinforcing their understanding of the symbolic language; if any of them did succeed in making gold in the literal sense, it was only a by-product of their own spiritual de-velopment, a by-product resulting from the analogy be-tween the microcosm and the macrocosm. The purpose of literally making gold in this way, was said to be to leave them free to pursue their spiritual lives without having recourse to base means of obtaining money on which to live, such as having to sink to the baseness of flattering a patron. The anonymous alchemical text known as 'The Glory of the World' says:

> "Let all your actions show that you love and fear God, and then every labour to which you set your hand will prosper, and from beginning to end you will pursue your work successfully and joyously..."

There were, of course, other alchemists who were purely and simply out for gold, and who did not understand the profound meaning of the science; they were given the name of 'puffers' because of their constant preoccupation with the alchemical furnace; they gave rise to the empiri-cists, who were the forerunners of the modern chemists.

William Law, the seventeenth century English mystic, wrote:

> "When Behmen first appeared in English, many per-sons of this nation, of the greatest wit and abilities, became his readers; who, instead of entering into his only one design, which was their own regeneration from an earthly to an heavenly life, turned chemists and set up furnaces to regenerate metals, in search of the philosopher's stone."

We have tried to demonstrate above that there are many different ways, both exoteric and esoteric, and that this diversity is simply a result of there being many different types of people who think and speak each in their own way. Our purpose in reviewing different ways in this book is to provide understanding, and a context within which the old legends may be better understood; it is not aimed at pointing out, or recommending, any specific way. Until quite modern times, the ways comprised in the great world religions and traditions each corresponded with particular ethnic groups, in some cases with a limited amount of overlap. They each existed with a fair amount of geographical isolation. Many who adhere to a particular tradition or religion believe it to be the best, or the only true one, while some of the great saints and sages have seen the transcendent unity of them all. The photographs on the next page are of one and the same tree as seen from each of the four points of the compass, four points of view; they show how one and the same thing may appear different according to the view of the onlooker. To take this analogy further, let us consider a great mountain such as Everest. A description of it as seen from Tibet, in the North, would have some points of similarity and many differences, when compared with one made from the South, in Nepal. Likewise, an account of the routes to be followed to climb the mountain from the North, would be quite different from one describing possible routes from the South. The great religions can thus be described as the same truth seen from different points of view; points of view or perspectives which are appropriate to the ways of thinking of different sections of humanity. We must add, however, that the analogies we have used may be adequate to convey an idea, but they are not perfect. The asymmetrical tree must not be taken as implying asymmetry in the truth behind religions; the image of climbing a mountain should not be taken in the modern sense of 'conquering' it as an individual achievement:

"To reach this lofty summit was given to me by God and nature." (Abraham Lambspring).

Another way of looking at religions is to take the traditional view of history. According to ancient sources, there was once a single humanity, with a single Primordial Tradition and language. The Chinese situate this first humanity on the Pamir*, a plateau to the West of Tibet; other traditions describe it as 'polar,' which can refer to a spiritual 'pole' - a link with Heaven - as well as one of

*According to Matgioi.

3. A tree photographed from different angles.

the earth's poles. Eventually the human race migrated outwards from this centre, in different directions. With the passage of time, language and culture came to differ. The role of the sages and prophets who have been instrumental in founding new religions in response to these changes, has not so much been to bring a 'new' religion in the literal sense, as to clothe or 'dress up' the Primordial Tradition in a form to suit the people of their times. This is true even for the revealed religions, for the purpose of the Divine Revelation was to bring about such an adaptation. Nicholas of Cusa, the German-born fifteenth century Roman Catholic philosopher, wrote:

> "Hence there is a single religion and a single creed for all beings endowed with understanding, and this religion is presupposed behind all the diversity of rites."

Thus, the Primordial Tradition is still hidden in the centre of each religion, and that is why we can speak of a perennial philosophy. That is also why there is a transcendent unity of religions, and why similar elements occur in different religions. Many of those who have made comparisons of religions without this point of view, have seen similar elements as 'borrowings.' For example, some German orientalists have seen Sufism as a borrowing from Hinduism, whereas the Sufis see their doctrine at the very centre of Islam. No doubt there are occasional instances of borrowings, like the example of Dante and Islam quoted earlier, but many traditional similarities are better understood in terms of common descent from a Primordial Tradition.

Before modern times, it was of little importance if people did not understand this transcendent unity of religions, for they were largely living in isolation and had their own way, a way which seemed 'right' to them. In the modern world, however, with its mixing of cultures and dissemination of information, it has become important for people to try to understand other ways.

Apart from prejudices which become ingrained at a very early age in people born into a religion, there is, in the West, a linguistic problem: We call the divine beings of the oriental and pre-Christian western pantheons 'Gods' and the supreme being of the monotheistic religions God. This use of the same word has led to many westerners seeing monotheism and polytheism as opposed and mutually contradictory. In fact, the 'Gods' of any polytheistic pantheon represent aspects of being, divine attributes, and they should be equated with the Heavenly hierarchies of saints and angels. A contradiction only arises between the two points of view when a polytheistic religion is becoming old, and a 'God' is given a quasi-absolute status, which is heretical because an attribute cannot be the whole. Many of the old Celtic legends, such as those collected in Brittany by Luzel, have suffered from the misunderstanding mentioned above, and the Pagan Gods in them have sometimes been changed into demons or giants, instead of divine attributes.

To those who would, on seeing the underlying unity, wish to fuse all into one, we quote the words of Abbot Minzing, a Buddhist:

> "Would the world be more beautiful if all the flowers on earth had been blended into one uniform colour, or all the mountains raised to make the earth monotonously flat? Each religion offers something glorious, peculiarly its own."

An old friend once said that the trouble with religions today is that the Catholics are worshipping Catholicism, the Muslims are worshipping Islam, etc. Religion is about man's relationship with God, or, in non-anthropomorphic terms, a Superior Principle. God, or the Principle, is the end in view; each religion is a means, not an end in itself.

CHAPTER 4. HEAVEN, HELL, AND REINCARNATION.

The western religions of Semitic origin, Judaism, Christianity, and Islam, tend to depict the posthumous states of Heaven and Hell as two starkly-opposed alternatives; two extremes with little between them. The oriental traditions, on the other hand, envisage a wide range of in-between possibilities, including reincarnation, both human and non-human. Christianity has tended to compress these in-between possibilities into a single idea of Purgatory where the soul undergoes a fixed period of penitence. Dante placed the Mountain of Purgatory at the antipodes of Jerusalem, whereas the Breton Tradition, as reported by Anatole Le Braz, describes defunct souls as doing their penitence in hollow trees or amongst gorse bushes in the countryside near their former homes. In Islam, the in-between possibilities are compressed into the idea of the 'punishment of the grave.' Modern Westerners who still profess a religion, tend to see Hell as eternal, in the sense of 'forever and ever,' and also as inescapable, once the soul has gone there. These are extreme views; the eternity of Hell should be seen as a time-cycle; it may be a very long time indeed in relation to a human life-span. In the Islamic Tradition it is said that 'at the end of time the fires of Hell will grow cold, and green grass will grow.' There is also an Islamic story of a man's soul which cried out to God above all the tumult of Hell, and God told them to pull him out, all blackened, and transfer him to a better place. We have already seen how a Christian writer, Dante, had Trajan rescued from Hell, and saved. The difference between our earthly state, and that represented by Hell, is that the former has almost infinitely more degrees of freedom than the latter. In this context, we should add that the inscription on Dante's gate of Hell reads: 'Give up all hope, you who enter.' In this life, conditions are very much better, and the spiritual possibilities, difficult as they may seem, are very much easier and greater than in the stronghold of Hell, from where spiritual escape is a very rare thing indeed.

In Western Europe, from the times of the Druids and right through the Middle Ages, there was a well-developed cult of the dead, based on the belief that the living could perform rites beneficial to them. In Britain, Archbishop Cranmer began the suppression of the cult of the dead by saying that they were either saved or lost and that was the end of it. Elsewhere in the West, the cult slowly decayed and became largely forgotten; it probably survived longest in Brittany.

The idea that Heaven and Hell are just single states of being is not borne out by the visionaries of both Islam and Christianity. Before Ibn 'Arabi and Dante, there were several Irish-Celtic saints who had detailed visions of Heaven and Hell. They included St Fursa (or Fursey), St Tundal, and St Adhamnan.

St Fursa probably came from Munster, and lived between 570 and 650 A.D., or thereabouts. In his first vision, his soul was taken out of his body and, in the company of three angels, he saw and heard the praises of the Heavenly Hosts. Three days later, he left his body once more, but this time his passage was delayed by demons who argued with his angels that he could not go forwards to eternal life because of his sins, the chief of which was vindictiveness. The angels answered the demons' arguments, and then Fursa became surrounded with a great brightness where he saw many saints and angels flying about. Next he came to a serene region where there were four angelic choirs, and where he received instruction before being returned to his body. His visions became well-known because Bede mentioned them in his Ecclesiastical History.

St Tundal seems also to have come from Munster. His vision was written down in Latin in 1149. It quickly became popular and was translated into many European languages. The vision happened when Tundal fell into a trance whilst visiting a friend in Cork. The trance lasted from Wednesday till the following Saturday. He later related his vision to one Marcus, who wrote it down. As soon as his soul left his body, he became greatly afraid, and hordes of demons surrounded him, taunting him and clawing at his face. Then a bright light approached - his guardian angel - who bade him 'welcome from God.' He followed his angel, seeing the sufferings of various categories of souls in Hell. Tundal's vision differs from most of the others, because he was not only taken on a guided tour of Hell, but also obliged to sample some of its torments himself. In one place they came to a horrible monster which was devouring dead souls; his guardian angel left him in its mouth where demons drove him down into its belly, but eventually he found himself outside again. Another time, they reached a lake full of monsters, with a narrow bridge over it. Thieves had to cross the bridge laden in proportion to their booty. Tundal had once stolen a cow, so he had to carry its weight over the bridge; he managed not to fall off, and reached the other side with his feet all cut and bleeding. Next he was chopped to bits by demons in a burning house, but at length he found himself outside and whole again. His last gruesome adventure in Hell was a visit to Lucifer in the nethermost parts.

On leaving Hell they came to a place of light where there were souls suffering hunger and thirst, and exposed to wind and rain. Then, a somewhat better place where the souls had, however, to purge themselves in fire for three hours each day. Both of these states add up to an idea of Purgatory.

Finally, Tundal had a vision of nine orders of Heaven, starting with a realm of the saints, crossing a wall of silver and then one of gold, through increasing glory, and ending with a vision of a tree laden with fruit and blossom of all kinds, the Tree of Life. Then he was returned to his body.

Tundal's vision develops the idea of Purgatory, and it shows Irish, perhaps Pagan-Irish influence on a Christian theme.

St Adhamnan likewise was conducted out of his body by his guardian angel. First, they came to the outer circle of the Bright Land of the Saints. There was a circle of fire surrounding it, but the saints passed in and out of it unscathed. Within the circle there was a Heavenly City with seven concentric walls of crystal, each one higher than the one before it. In the centre was the Throne of God. Everywhere there was light, sweet music, and perfume. Such, in brief, was Adhamnan's vision of Heaven. The crystal walls of the Heavenly City are interesting, for some of Luzel's tales from Brittany show the pagan Sun-God as living in a crystal palace.

Adhamnan referred to souls in Purgatory both in this world, on heights and in marshy places, and outside the heavenly gate, which they were prevented from passing by clashing veils of fire and ice. In his vision, all the souls of the dead had first to pass through the Heavenly City for their meeting with God. Those of the good passed easily; those of the wicked were burnt in fires above each

4. Dante (D) and Beatrice (B) near the starry heaven
(after the 1491 edition of the Divina Comedia).

of the doors of the concentric city walls, before passing to the next. Finally they reached God and received their judgment.

Adhamnan's vision also included a guided tour of Hell where he saw the hideous sufferings and torments allotted to different classes of the damned. He also saw, beyond the land of torment, a fiery wall which was the abode of demons alone. His vision of Hell included some islands set in a fiery lake; and the islands had walls of silver around them which protected their inhabitants somewhat. The latter were said to be those who, although they were not saved, had been generous and given alms to the poor. This stresses the question of degree, or relativity in Hell, in sharp contrast to the single fire-and-brimstone version of many fundamentalists.

We have looked at the visions of these Irish saints in some detail, partly because of the Celtic leaning of this book, and partly because Dante's vision may already be well known to most of our readers. Furthermore, we have already commented on Dante in an earlier chapter. His Divine Comedy is without doubt one of the finest poems in history. His vision itself has a beautiful symmetry, showing the circles of Heaven and Hell disposed in hier-archical sequence around a central pole or axis, and Hell something of an inverse reflection of Heaven. Dante's ex-panding vision of ascent through ever increasing Heavenly circles suddenly changes, in the Empyrean (Tenth Heaven) to a centripetal vision of the Snow White Rose of Paradise - the Divinity with surrounding angels in the form of a flower calyx - reminiscent of a chalice or the grail. The extent to which Dante was influenced by the Celtic vision-aries is not so clear, however, as his link with Ibn 'Arabi's 'Meccan Revelations.'

Now we turn from Heaven, Hell, and Purgatory, to the idea of reincarnation. We know very little of the religion of the pre-Christian Celts. Caesar gives us to understand that the Druids taught survival of the soul, and its pas-sage from one body to another. Another classical writer, Diodorus, implied that the Celts believed that the soul, after a fixed number of years, entered into a second body. However, it is not absolutely clear if Diodorus is referring directly to Celtic teachings, or comparing them with the Pythagorean doctrine. Christianity only declared officially against the doctrine of reincarnation at the

Council of Constantinople, in 543 A.D. The sixth century Welsh poem attributed to Taliesin still implies such an idea:

"I have been in Asia with Noah in the ark,
I have seen the destruction of Sodom and Gomorrah,
I was in India when Rome was built,
I have now come here to the remnant of Troia*.

Then was I for nine months
In the womb of the witch Ceridwen
I was originally little Gwion
And at length I am Taliesin."

There is also an Irish legend, said to have been told by Tuan Mac Cairill to St Finnen, and which implies rebirth in animal, as well as human form. According to the legend Tuan Mac Cairill said that he was once a man who, at the age of 100 years, fell asleep. He woke up to find himself a stag, in which form he lived 80 years; then a boar for 20 years, a vulture for 100 years, and a fish for 20 years. The fish, a salmon, was caught, cooked and eaten. Then he was born again as a human in the Mac Cairill family. Although some writers have given this legend a shamanistic interpretation, the long period of time spent in each form, and the reference to birth through a human womb, would imply more the idea of reincarnation. The Buddha similarly recalled his previous lives which were spent in animal form.

Religious 'truths' are not so much total truths, as saving truths. The truths of the western revealed religions are spiritual ones; nowhere, for example, did God bother to mention that the world was round, and not flat. If the Christian denial of the doctrine of reincarnation was perhaps not strictly or universally correct, it may have protected many Westerners from their own imaginations. Furthermore, as a 'truth' it was a decision of a Council, perhaps 'inspired,' but not part of the direct Christian revelation. The reason for the Christian denial of this doctrine may be seen in the difference between oriental and western attitudes to it: The Oriental reacts by saying "what must I do to escape from this endless chain of

*A reference to the mythical Trojan ancestry of the Britons.

38

births and deaths?" whereas many Westerners react by an imaginative preoccupation with what they might have been in a previous life. How many Westerners taken with this idea have wasted their time imagining that they were Henry VIII or one of his wives?

One advantage offered by the theory of reincarnation is that it gives the idea of a life prior to this one. Such an idea helps one to understand why people sometimes suffer out of proportion to sins they have committed in this life. In this vein, Apuleius wrote that the Gods consider the soul's various existences as a whole, and sometimes punish it for sins committed during a previous life. The fact that someone is seen as being punished by God should not be an excuse for not practising virtue towards that person, but quite the contrary. Even in an ordinary learning situation, we all make mistakes which cause us problems, but we often equally help one another through such difficulties, rather than blame one another.

The Tibetan Book of the Dead gives us a fascinating vision from the time of death until that of rebirth. It reads like an adventure story. According to this work, the soul of a dead person takes three and a half days before realizing that it is dead. During this period, it can hear what is going on around it*. The book goes on to say that when the soul leaves the body, it can move anywhere at will, and see and hear without being seen and heard itself. If it does not obtain deliverance, or salvation, and does not slip into one of the Hells, then there remain for it the possibilities of being born again, or becoming a wandering ghost. The book warns the soul to avoid this last possibility. The soul destined to be born again comes to be driven by psychic forces towards its destiny, and its memory of its former life begins to fade. If the new existence is likely to be animal, the soul sees visions of brown earth with holes in it; if it is destined to be born a human, it has different visions according to the region of the earth where it will take place. The book advises against being born in the West on the grounds that religion is weakest there. When a soul is close to being born in human form, it sees a couple making love; if the

*If this is true, modern practices of dealing with corpses, including their isolated storage in refrigerated drawers, must, to say the least, be far from beneficial to the souls who may not even realize they are dead.

soul loves the mother and hates the father, it will, according to the book, be born male; if it hates the mother and loves the father, it will be born female. Then the soul enters the womb (and therefore, according to the Tibetan Book of the Dead, the unborn child has a soul from the time of conception). Those who smile at the ideas related by the Tibetans should consider the possibility that they may have put as much effort into their inquiry as modern man has in developing the micro-chip, or sending rockets to the moon.

The idea of reincarnation should not be seen as contradicting any notions in the western religions of the soul sleeping until the Day of Judgment. An affirmation of one of these ideas does not necessarily exclude or contradict the others; Zhuang Zi, the great Daoist sage of China, recognized reincarnation, but also the idea of souls sleeping in 'the great dormitory between Heaven and Earth.' Perhaps at this late stage of the present cycle, the possibilities for being born again are restricted; Black Elk, the North American Indian whose great vision is referred to elsewhere in this book, also had one of colossal numbers of baby-faced souls waiting to be born on earth.

CHAPTER 5. THE SPIRITUAL JOURNEY; KILLING THE INWARD DRAGON.

From the point of view of exoterism, the superior states represented collectively by Heaven can only be considered as belonging to the angelic beings, or as states that may be achieved after death. Esoterism, on the other hand, sees the superior states as attainable even during this life, before the death of the body.

The Doctrine of the Fall implies that man has lost something which was once his by right, or which, in primordial times, was easily accessible to him. The first part of the way invloves a return to the primordial state of True Man, after which the true spiritual journey commences, through the superior states often represented symbolically by the Heavens, and ending in Divine Union*. The first part of the way ends in 'salvation;' the final end is 'deliverance.' The famous dance of the seven veils symbolises the spiritual journey. The shedding of the first veil represents the Primordial State; as each subsequent veil is shed, the observer sees a further increase in beauty, until finally, with the last, the naked truth of the Seventh Heaven is revealed in all its glory.

The first part of the way, the return to the state of True Man, involves the crossing of the 'lower waters' of Genesis, the dangerous realm of the psyche. In the classical traditions of antiquity, this first part of the journey was called the 'lesser mysteries.' This first part of the way ends in a death - of the ego, the inward dragon or beast - and a rebirth** as True Man. Rebirth can be described as an unveiling of what was already there, but which was hidden or imprisoned by the previous state. True man is master of himself, no longer pushed around by his ego; as master of himself he can truly be called a king, the vice-regent of God on earth. Sometimes True Man is described as a New Man, as opposed to the Old Man. When Sindbad the Sailor shook the Old Man of the

*As a matter of interest, the equivalent of the Hindu word for Divine Union, Yoga, can still be found in English - the word yoke - that which unites the oxen to the plough!
**This rebirth is difficult to achieve and not all can go that far. It cannot be attained as easily as some 'twice-born,' instant Christians would have us believe.

5. Killing the dragon
(after Walter Crane wood engraving).

Sea off his back, he smashed him with a rock, saying may God have no mercy on him; for the Old Man, the false ego, is an illusion. This idea of death and rebirth is to be found everywhere:

"Die before you die." (Muhammad).
"No creature can attain a higher grade of nature without ceasing to exist." (St Thomas Aquinas).
"The substance is destroyed in a bath and its parts reunited by putrefaction. In ashes it blossoms." (Basil Valentine, the famous alchemist).
"The destruction of one thing is the generation of another." (The Glory of the World).
"And through this spiritual dying... all his actions have a heavenly source, and no longer seem to belong to this earth. For he lives no longer according to the flesh, but according to the spirit... in works that stand the test of fire." (The Sophic Hydrolith).

Richard Cavendish, in King Arthur and the Grail, describes the knightly aim in this context, as the conquest of death. The Delphic inscription said: 'Know thyself.' The Hindus regard this death of the ego as the death of the self with a small 's,' as opposed to the true Self, with a capital 'S.' Lao Zi, the Old Master of the Daoists said: "Knowing others is wisdom, but knowing oneself* is superior wisdom." This first stage can be described symbolically as a hazardous and difficult journey to a 'place,' and also towards one's own spiritual centre. The root of the English verb to navigate is related to the Sanskrit *nabis,* meaning the umbilicus, so that the symbolism of navigation is of returning to one's primordial centre.

Traditionally, in the human microcosm, the heart is described as the spiritual centre - not the pumping organ in the chest - but what it symbolises. In an earlier chapter we pointed out that the language of many ancient crafts is at one and the same time practical and symbolic. In traditional boat building, the boat is seen like a human body lying face upwards; the keel represents both the backbone and the lowest part, and along the inside of the keel we find the hog - symbolic of the lowest element in man. A stem and stern are fitted to the front and rear of the keel assembly, a series of ribs laterally, and the hull is planked. From the top of the stem, a king plank

*One's true Self.

runs backwards about a third of the length of the boat, where it is supported by a Samson-post set vertically above the keel. At the point of intersection of Samson-post and king plank, a tabernacle is constructed to take the mast. The tabernacle can be seen as representing the heart as spiritual centre, the mast as the spiritual axis between it and Heaven.

In the army hierarchy we have the ranks of private, corporal, captain, and colonel, the highest regimental officer. The word colonel is derived from the Italian *colonello* (Latin *colonna*) meaning a column, which can imply the spiritual axis; it came via the French, where it was at first spelt *coronel*, either by accident or design. It is perhaps no accident that this word is pronounced similar to the kernel, the vital centre of the fruit, and the French word *coeur*, meaning heart. The colonel therefore corresponds with the spiritual element in man, seen as the heart and spiritual axis*. There may also be a link with the Latin *corona*, meaning crown, associated with the idea of True Man as king. (Similarly, in anatomy, the coronary artery is associated with the heart). When words are chosen for a particular purpose, they are not always selected on a basis of their linguistic derivation, but on one of association of ideas from their sounds. The captain, from the cap on the head, represents the brain, or mental faculty; the corporal, the physical or corporeal body, with its appetites and needs; and the private, the private parts, sexual desire**. Fallen man does not know his own heart as his spiritual centre. His mental faculty has its limits; it is subject to uncontrolled wanderings of the imagination, and the nagging of bodily and sexual desires, which frequently take control. The attainment of the state of primordial man represents a restoration of the true hierarchy represented by colonel-captain-corporal-private, in which the spirit controls the mind, which in turn con-

*The Hindus have a science called 'nirukta' which claims that there are often meaningful relationships between similar sounding words even when there is no etymological link. The Hindus also link the heart with the crown and the solar ray (cf. spiritual axis).
**Some modern readers may be prejudiced against any idea of hierarchy, perhaps through experience of inferior people holding rank. Throughout this book, references to rank or grade should be understood in terms of the qualities they represent, without reference to particular persons.

trols the bodily and sexual appetites. This does not so much mean that sex is the lowest element, but that as the strongest it needs the greatest degree of control. On the corporeal level, the pure and unperverted sexual act symbolises Divine Union. The total inversion of the spirit-mind-body-sex hierarchy represents Hell; we shall return to this point in chapter 10.

A similar symbolism is to be found in Wu Ch'eng-en's Chinese classic, the story of Monkey. In the first part of the tale, Monkey 'plays Hell' on earth and in Heaven. Monkey represents the brain or mental faculty; the trouble he causes is due to his being isolated from the Spirit. He is punished for this for a time. In the second part of the story he sets out on a pilgrimage to the Buddha, accompanied by a priest named Tripitaka, a horse called Sandy, and a pig. Tripitaka represents the self about to be reborn as the true Self; the horse and pig represent the body, appetite, and sexual desire. On their pilgrimage they come to a river which they have to cross on a ferry; the death of the self is aptly described in the following passage:

> "The ferryman punted them dextrously out from the shore. Suddenly they saw a body in the water, drifting rapidly downstream. Tripitaka stared at it in consternation. Monkey laughed. 'Dont be frightened, Master,' he said. 'That's you.' And Pigsy said 'It's you, it's you.' Sandy clapped his hands. 'It's you, it's you,' he cried. The ferryman joined in the chorus. 'There you go,' he cried. 'My best congratulations.'"

In terms of heart symbolism, the return to the primordial state of True Man, the first part of the way, or the accomplishment of the 'lesser mysteries,' is described as a return to the outside of the heart. The spiritual journey proper, the 'greater mysteries,' is then a journey to the centre of the heart.

Often this first part of the way is described in terms of holy warfare. The Bhagavad Gita, the great Hindu work on karma-yoga says that a man is his own friend when he has conquered himself by the Self; but when his self is unconquered, it acts like his own enemy. Sometimes the self that must be overcome is represented as a beast within - an inward dragon - which must be killed. This is why mediaeval knights are often depicted with a beast be-

6. Knight with lion.

neath their feet. Abraham Lambspring, the alchemist described in the Hermetic Museum as 'a noble ancient philosopher,' wrote:

> "The Sage says that a wild beast is in the forest, whose skin is of blackest dye. If any man cut off his head, his blackness will disappear, and give place to snowy white."

This killing of the inward beast is the norm on the spiritual way. There is, however, the rare possibility of taking things a step further, taming the beast, and making use of its power. This may explain why some statues of the Buddha show him with the coils of a cobra beneath his feet, but with its head raised up protectively above his own. A similar symbolism occurs also in some Hindu folktales.

Sometimes the beast within is given a dual aspect. Abraham Lambspring wrote:

> "The Sages do faithfully teach us that two strong Lions, to wit male and female, lurk in the dark and rugged valley*. These the Master must catch. Though they are swift and fierce, and of terrible and savage aspect, he who by wisdom and cunning can secure and bind them, and lead them into the same forest, of him it may be said with justice and truth, that he has merited the meed of praise before all others, and that his wisdom transcends that of the worldly wise."

Similarly, Hermes, who represents the priestly wisdom of Egyptian antiquity, says:

> "The soul must begin by warring against itself, and stirring up within itself a mighty feud and the one part of the soul must win victory over the others, which are more in number. It is a feud of one against two, the one part struggling to mount upward, and the other two dragging it down; and there is much strife and fighting between them. And it makes no small difference whether the one side or the other

*The dark valley of the soul.

47

wins, for the one part strives towards the Good, the others make their home among evils; the one yearns for freedom, the others are content with slavery. And if the two parts are vanquished, they stay quiet in themselves, and submissive to the ruling part*; but if the one part is defeated, it is carried off as a captive by the two, and the life it lives on earth is a life of penal torment. Such is the contest about the journey to the world above. You must begin, my son, by winning victory in this contest, and then, having won, mount upwards**."

Once, the way to the primordial state of True Man, and beyond, was direct. In historical times it has become indirect. Dante began by trying a direct route, but he found his way blocked by a she-wolf; he was informed that the way he was trying was closed, and that the only way open was via the centre of Hell - hence the idea of the descent into Hell - as seen in the spiritual journey, and in the lives of prophets and saints. At the very centre of Hell, Dante saw his guide place his head where his feet were, and vice-versa. He did likewise and found he was ready to make the ascent out of Hell. The literal interpretation is simply that downwards becomes upwards as one passes through the very centre of the earth; but the deeper meaning is that at the centre of Hell the spirit-mind-body-sex hierarchy is inverted. In other words, the being at the centre of Hell is inverted with reference to this hierarchy, but it can be corrected by simply turning itself upside-down.

Although Dante's experience was described as a vision, and St Tundal's occurred during a trance, one should not gain the impression that the descent into hell, into the dark depths of the soul, is simply a matter of a brief experience in a dream-like state. In fact, the descent into Hell may be a 'real' experience here and now on this earth, which for the seeker becomes one of Hell on earth. In the Koran it is written that God is the First, the Last, the Outward, and the Inward. Because of the analogy be-

*In other words, it is more a question of defeating and subduing the inward beasts, than of killing them.
**This victory represents the 'lesser mysteries;' mounting upwards, the 'greater mysteries.'

tween the microcosm (of oneself) and the macrocosm (of the world around us), Hell can be experienced as an inward vision or as the world around us seeming everywhere to turn against us, with no means of escape and no apparent remedy, remaining similarly hostile even if we rush from one place to another. Shaikh Darqawi, a Moroccan Sufi Master, said that of these four Divine Manifestations, the Outward is the most difficult to understand. The Outward sometimes becomes a manifestation of Hell for two reasons: Firstly, as part of the spiritual journey, it can represent a process of Divine Alchemy designed to purge and purify the being; secondly, it can occur because the seeker must learn to recognize the Spirit in all its manifestations, including those which seem unpleasant, and not try to run away from it or seek some worldly remedy. From this second point of view, the experience of Hell on earth is in a sense a test of faith, to see if the seeker will keep to his or her spiritual method even in the face of adversity, and continue on the spiritual path, come what may. This can be further explained by the analogy of holy warfare: What would a leader think of a warrior who performed well during training exercises, but ran away as soon as the enemy appeared?

In an earlier chapter we have indicated the wide variety of ways, each leading to the attainment of the state of True Man, and beyond. Whatever the way, it can be summarised as discernment of the true from the false, the real from the illusory - in moral terms, good from evil - and concentrating on the true, real, or good. The false, illusory, or evil can be described as the 'world' - not the world in itself, but the world seen as 'real' and 'separate' by our own self, which forms attachments to it, and tries to appropriate it - and likewise our own self, which is false because it does not know its own true Self. The true or real can be described as the ultimate being, God, The One, or, going beyond being, the Most High God, in non-anthropomorphic terms, the Principle, the Absolute. Because God is the First, the Last, the Outward, and the Inward, the spiritual centre can be conceived as outside ourselves, 'above,' and beyond time; it can also be conceived as within ourselves. If we recognize the spirit as within ourselves, we must also recognize it as within other beings, and if we do so, this makes the practice of virtue in our relationships with them another important part of the way, as well as the discernment mentioned above. Not to practise virtue in our lives, is to deny the Spirit in one of its manifestations. (In the West, with the rise of individualism, the custom of bowing to others has almost disappeared; it still persists to some extent in the East. When a true Oriental bows before another person, he is not lowering himself before that person's individuality, which may be unpleasant, but bowing to the Spirit concealed within).

Having summarised the mystical way as a discernment between true and false, and the practice of virtue, there remains, in relation to concentration on the true, the question of method. In the ancient world a wide range of methods existed. They included mental*, or rational dialectic methods which aimed at breaking through from the purely rational to the supra-rational and spiritual. In some Zen schools in the Far East, the disciple was suddenly confronted with a mental shock - something non-rational or enigmatic - which would make the break-through for him; in other cases a physical shock at the correct moment could produce the same effect. Many other methods come under the headings of contemplation or meditation. In many active ways, external life also played an important role, because of the analogy between the microcosm and the macrocosm, and the need for virtue. Contemplation can be linked with intelligence, the Spirit; meditation with reason. The highest form of contemplation consists in totally emptying oneself so that the mind and imagination are completely still and the being is like a clean, empty vessel, open at the top to receive the influx of Heaven. Meditation can be focussed on an object; it can also take the form of what the Hindus call mantra-yoga, the repetition of a Sacred Phrase or Name. The practice of meditation can eventually lead to a state of true contemplation in which the being becomes one with the object of the meditation. In the Manava Dharma

---

*In modern times a purely mental approach to spirituality is unlikely to take one beyond a limited theoretical understanding. It is perhaps no accident that the French have a related verb 'mentir,' meaning to tell lies (cf. English mendacity) and implying that if one relies too much on one's mental faculty - if one makes a best friend of it - it can let one down. Christ's betrayal by one of his own disciples - one of his best friends - illustrates this idea.

Shastra, or Laws of Manu, which purports to have been formulated in the age prior to this one, a disciple asks his Master about the future Age of Kali, the Iron Age. The Master comments on it as a time of warfare, suffering, and superstition, adding that of the various spiritual methods then available, only mantra-yoga (the repetition of a Sacred Phrase or Name) will be effective. The reason given is that humanity will have changed so much that only mantra-yoga* will be suitable.

The difficulty of meditation comes from the restlessness of the mental faculty. Monkey, whom we have already described as representing this faculty, said:

> "If it were just a matter of playing football with the firmament, stirring up the ocean, turning back rivers, carrying away mountains... Even if it were a question of... any kind of transference or transformation, I would take on the job at once... but if it comes to sitting still and meditating, I am bound to come off badly. It's quite against my nature to sit still."

Mantra can go hand in hand with the active life of karma-yoga, the way of destiny achieved by following a vocation. The Manava Dharma Shastra can thus be seen as recommending an active way for the end of the Age of Kali.

Mantra-yoga has its counterparts in other traditions. In Islam it is known as *Dhikr Llah*, the remembrance of God, and it ranges from the repetition of the whole of the Koran, through sacred phrases of which the best known is *Llah illa-ha illa-Llah***, to the repetition of the Divine Name of Majesty, *Allah*. In Orthodox Christianity there is

---

*The Hari Krishna Mantra is thus recommended in Orthodox Hinduism as **the** method for the present time. Its adoption in the West may, however have its limitations; few Westerners are mentally pre-adapted to accomodate themselves to a Hindu context, and many of the western converts have become highly proselyte, something quite foreign to the Hindus, who, until very modern times, have never sought to convert the rest of the world.

**Llah illa-ha illa-Llah is the first part of the shahadah, or testimony of faith, in Islam; it can be transliterated as 'no God if not God.' It cannot, in fact, be translated adequately by a single phrase, but the sense is that God is the only reality, truth, etc.

the prayer of the heart, made famous in the West by the anonymous work called 'The Way of a Pilgrim.' A brief passage from it will give an idea of the fruits of the method:

> "The prayer of my heart gave me such consolation that I felt there was no happier person on earth than I, and I doubted if there could be fuller and greater happiness in the Kingdom of Heaven. Not only did I feel this in my own soul, but the whole outside world also seemed to me full of charm and delight... Sometimes I felt as light as though I had no body and was floating through the air instead of walking. Sometimes when I withdrew into myself, I... was filled with wonder at the wisdom with which the human body is made."

Mantra-yoga, or its equivalent in other traditions, has the advantage that it gives the mind something on which to concentrate, for, as we have pointed out, it is not its nature to be still. Practice can, however, lead to inner stillness and a state of contemplation. The method has the further advantage that, although it generally requires periodic withdrawn meditative practice, it can also be practised during much of the active life. As a method linked with an active life, it is, in a sense, closer to the ways of primordial times than are others, such as ascetic monasticism. Religion, such as we know it, probably did not exist in primordial times, because the people of those times had the thing in question within themselves. A way of internal invocation in an active life can thus be seen as the closest possible approach to the ancient primordial ways. This is perhaps one of the reasons why monasticism is forbidden in Islam, which, as the last revealed religion of this cycle of humanity, shows some correspondence to the beginning.

We know next to nothing of the methods used by the knights of old. When we read, however, of their setting forth "in the name of God," we should remember that this is no empty phrase, and that, apart from implying that they did everything in the name of God, it probably also implies that they went forth with some internal invocatory method equivalent to mantra-yoga.

Whatever the way, past or present, the disciple is normally initiated into it, and given a method, by a Master*. The need for this is twofold: Firstly, the spiritual life is the most difficult of all, and frequent guidance is necessary; secondly, some methods, such as the direct invocation of a Name of God, for example the name *Allah* mentioned above, involve a direct approach to Divine Majesty. This is best explained by analogy: If an ordinary citizen not versed in courtly ways, were to burst into a royal mediaeval court and address the king directly, he would almost certainly incur the kings displeasure; if, on the other hand, he were under the protection of a courtier and properly introduced into the court, no such displeasure would be incurred. Similarly, a direct approach to Divine Majesty by those unqualified, and without the protection of a Master, could provoke Divine Wrath. In the Gospel of St Matthew (VII, 22, 23) we read:

> "Many will say to me in that day, Lord, Lord, have we not prophesied in thy name? and in thy name have cast out devils? and in thy name done many wonderful works. And I will profess unto them, I never knew you: depart from me, ye that work iniquity."

There are, however, other forms of mantra or its equivalent which are less direct; the invocation of the first part, or the whole of the Shahadah seems to be open to all in Islam; likewise the rosary for Christians.

In the next few chapters we shall look at stories of the Arthurian quest, with some explanatory introductions and footnotes, but we hope the reader will have sufficient background from the first part of this book to draw some conclusions of his, or her own.

*For an idea of the role of a great Spiritual Master see 'The Life of Milarepa, Tibet's Great Sage,' whose Master was Marpa. For an example of the teaching of a great Islamic Master, see 'Letters of a Sufi Master' (Shaikh Darqawi).

CHAPTER 6. THE LOVE-QUEST.

We have already pointed out that a way of love is one of the three basic mystical, or esoteric paths. 'As there is wedlock between a man and wife, so there is wedlock between God and the soul,' said Eckhart. In its best-known form, such a way involves a contemplative or meditative approach to the Spirit; the lover is consumed inwardly as if by a raging fire of love; and at the end of the way, the lover is, as it were, consumed also from without, like a moth flying into the flame of a candle.

Love can, however, have something of a spiritual quality even when it is not intentionally and consciously turned towards God. True love of another person, when it is more than just infatuation or physical attraction, has a spiritual quality in so far as the lover thinks only of the beloved, with no thought of his, of her own self. This selfless quality in true love can lead towards a weakening, and even a virtual overcoming of the ego. This spiritual quality of true love, thus defined, applies also to those who devote themselves wholeheartedly and selflessly to a work of love, such as the care of the sick and dying. Love of others can, as we have already noted, be love of the Spirit within them.

A way of love, leading to the death of the self, is symbolised in some of the world's greatest love tragedies, in which two young people fall deeply in love in circumstances which prevent them from coming together in a permanent relationship, and which end in their apparently tragic death. In these tales we see a strong element of destiny; the pair cannot help falling in love, and seem to have been destined to do so, but circumstances prevent them from marrying and living together as is the normal course of lovers. They are thereby destined towards a love which transcends corporeal forms; a love which is spiritual rather than physical; a love which can lead to the contemplation of Divine Beauty:

'Did my heart love till now? forswear it sight!
For I ne'er saw true beauty till this night.*'

The tragic element is twofold; first, because their love

*Shakespeare, Romeo and Juliet, 1, v.

is like an internal raging fire, and second, because it ends in death. The latter is only tragic as seen in the literal interpretation of the story; the profound meaning is that their love has led to a death of the self, and salvation, or beyond.

Three of the greatest love tragedies which come to mind are Shakespeare's Romeo and Juliet, Nizami's Islamic tale of Layla and Majnun, and the story of Tristan and Isoude, which forms part of the Arthurian Cycle.

The story of Layla and Majnun is of a young couple who fall in love, but whose families are bitter enemies. When Majnun finds that all forms of persuasion fail, he enlists the help of his friends to go to war against Layla's family, with a view to taking her from them by force. When the fighting begins, Majnun's supporters become perplexed because he even weeps over the death of his enemies. Majnun therefore fails to take Layla by force; he becomes a desert hermit, living with the wild animals who become his friends and protectors. He spends his time composing love verses to his beloved, and those of his friends who visit him think he has gone crazy. The story ends with Majnun stretched out dying on the grave of his beloved, protected from interference by his friends, the lions.

Shakespeare no doubt knew the story of Tristan and Isoude. He seems, however, to have based his play of Romeo and Juliet more on the model of Layla and Majnun than on the former, perhaps because his Elizabethan audience wanted a change from the Arthurian romances, and perhaps also because he, like Dante, possibly had secret links with the Islamic world. Like Layla and Majnun, Romeo and Juliet has the theme of love thwarted by a family feud. The tragic ending of Romeo and Juliet does, however, have something in common with that of Tristan (or Tristram) and Isoude. We give the latter story as an example of the love tragedy:

Tristan and Isoude.

Meliadus was King of Lionesse, a country which adjoined the kingdom of Cornwall, but which has now disappeared beneath the ocean. Meliadus was married to Isabella, who was the sister of King Mark of Cornwall. One day, when Meliadus was out hunting, a fairy fell in love with him and drew him away by enchantment. Queen Isabella set out in

7. Tristan hunting with his bow
(Chertsey tile)

search of him, but was taken ill on the journey. She gave birth to a son whom she called Tristan, because of the sad circumstances in which he was born*; then she died.

Gouvernail, the queen's squire, who had accompanied her, took the child to his father, who had managed to break the fairy's enchantments and return home.

Seven years later, Meliadus married again. The new queen grew jealous of Tristan, her stepson, and plotted to do away with him. Gouvernail heard of the plot and fled with the boy to the court of the King of France where they were welcomed and where Tristan grew up learning the arts and knightly accomplishments. He particularly distinguished himself above all other youths at the court with his knowledge of hunting. Belinda, the king's daughter, fell in love with him, but as Tristan did not return her passion, she turned her father against him, in a fit of anger. Tristan was banished from the kingdom; Belinda soon repented, and, after writing a tender letter to her loved one, killed herself. Gouvernail was afraid to take Tristan back to his native country because his father was dead and his stepmother now held the throne. He therefore took him to Cornwall, to his Uncle Mark, who gave him a kind reception.

King Mark lived in the castle at Tintagel. Tristan distingushed himself there in all the exercises incumbent on a knight, and he soon found an opportunity to show off his courage and skill. Moraunt, a famous champion and brother to the Queen of Ireland, arrived asking tribute of King Mark. The latter's knights were all afraid to bear arms against the Irishman, so Tristan begged his uncle to admit him to the order of knighthood, with a view to fighting the battle of Cornwall against the Irish champion. King Mark agreed reluctantly, conferred knighthood upon Tristan, and fixed a time and place for the encounter.

This combat was the first, and one of the most glorious of Tristan's exploits. The young knight, though severely wounded, managed to cleave Moraunt's head, leaving a piece of his sword in the wound. Moraunt was obliged to quit, and he hastened to his ship and sailed away with all speed to Ireland; he died soon after his arrival there.

*In the old Celtic tales, those destined to be great are often born in unusual circumstances, or conceived out of wedlock; in the latter case, sometimes the father is non-human.

8. Combat of Tristan with Moraunt
(Chertsey tile).

58

Thus the kingdom of Cornwall was delivered from its tribute. Sorely wounded, Tristan fell unconscious, and his friends rushed to his aid. They dressed his wounds, all but one of which healed normally. The tip of Moraunt's lance had been poisoned, and the wound it had inflicted grew worse day by day, no matter what remedy they tried, so Tristan asked his uncle for permission to seek a cure in Loegria (England). With his consent, he took ship, but contrary winds drove him to the coast of Ireland. He landed there, and, taking out his rote*, began to play on it. It was a summer evening and the King of Ireland and his daughter, the beautiful Isoude, were at the window overlooking the sea. They sent for the stranger musician who, realizing he was in Ireland and in danger from having recently slain its champion, introduced himself under a false name. The queen began to restore him to health, using a medicated bath, and, because of his artistic skill, they made him tutor of music and poetry to the princess. Under his tuition Isoude benefited so well that she became the best in the kingdom, except for her instructor.

During this time, a tournament was held and many of Arthur's knights were present. On the first day a Saracen prince, named Palamedes, won all the victories. The latter was therefore invited to court where they gave a feast. Tristan, who was also present at the feast, noticed how Palamedes had fallen for the fair Isoude, and how he made no secret of it. Tristan felt the pain of jealousy, which made him realize how much Isoude meant to him.

The tournament continued the following day. Although Tristan's wound was not yet fully healed, he armed himself in secret in the forest, and then mingled with the combatants. He overthrew everyone he encountered, including Palamedes, and won the day. His wound, however, reopened as a result of his exertions, and they carried him into the palace where the fair Isoude herself took on the task of caring for him. She soon restored him to good health.

It happened one day that one of the court damsels went into the closet where Tristan's armour was kept. Noticing that a bit of his sword had been broken off, it occurred to her that the missing piece was like the one they had taken from Moraunt's skull. She spoke of this to the

*A musical instrument.

59

9. Tristan singing to Isoude
(Chertsey tile).

queen, who compared Tristan's sword with the fragment taken from her brother's wound, and concluded that he was the one who had taken her brother's life. She complained to the king, who first went to see for himself, and then had Tristan cited before the whole court as one who had dared present himself before them after having slain their kinsman. Tristan admitted what he had done, adding that it was by force of wind and waves alone that he had reached their shores. The queen demanded the death penalty, which made the fair Isoude turn pale and tremble, but a murmur arose from the court for one so handsome and brave; generosity triumphed over resentment in the mind of the king, and he simply banished Tristan from the land, under pain of death.

Tristan, now restored to health, returned to Cornwall. King Mark made him recount his adventures in detail. Tristan accordingly told him all that had happened, but when he came to speak of fair Isoude, he could not help describing her as only a lover would. King Mark was fascinated by his description of her, and, biding his time, he asked a boon of his nephew. The latter readily agreed, and the king made him swear upon the holy relics that he would fulfil his command. Then Mark told him to go to Ireland and obtain for him the fair Isoude to be Queen of Cornwall.

Tristan believed it would be certain death for him to return to Ireland, yet, bound by oath, he could not hesitate. He took the precaution of changing his armour, and set sail for Ireland. This time contrary winds drove him to the coast of England, near Camelot, where King Arthur was holding his court, attended by the knights of the Round Table, and many others, the most illustrious in the world.

Tristan kept his identity secret. He took part in many jousts, in which he covered himself with glory. One day he saw the King of Ireland, Isoude's father, among those recently arrived. He had been accused of treason against his liege sovereign, Arthur, and he had come to Camelot to answer the charge. His accusor was Blaenor, one of the most formidable warriors of the Round Table, and Argius, the king, had neither youthful vigour nor strength to encounter him. He therefore needed a champion to fight for him and show his innocence, but the knights of the Round Table were not allowed to fight one another,

10. The King of Ireland
(Chertsey tile).

except in the matter of personal disputes. Argius heard of the unknown knight's prowess, and witnessed some of his exploits. He sought him out and asked him to act in his defence, swearing on oath that he was innocent of the accusation. Tristan readily agreed and made himself known to the king who, for his part promised that should he succeed, he might ask for any reward he wished.

Tristan fought Blaenor and threw him; the latter called on him to use his right of conquest and strike the fatal blow, but Tristan replied, 'God forbid that I should take the life of so brave a knight.' The judges decided that the King of Ireland was acquitted of the charge against him. King Argius invited Tristan to return with him to Ireland where he was welcomed even by the queen, in gratitude for saving her husband's life.

This was a happy moment for Isoude, but Tristan looked on her with despair, because of the cruel oath which bound him. In a trembling voice, he asked for the fair Isoude on behalf of his uncle.

Argius consented and they made preparations for the voyage. Brengwain, Isoude's favourite maid, was to go with her. On the day of departure, the queen took the maid aside and told her that she had procured a potent love-draught which should be administered to Isoude and King Mark on the evening of their wedding. This would ensure that her husband would treat her well and it would also protect her from her attachment to Tristan.

Isoude, Tristan and Brengwain set sail with a favourable wind. The lovers gazed at each other, sighing. It was a warm day, and Isoude complained she was thirsty. Tristan spotted the bottle containing the love-potion, which the maid had forgotten to hide out of sight. He gave some of it to Isoude, and drank the rest himself; his dog licked the cup dry. They reached Cornwall and Isoude was married to King Mark. The old monarch was delighted with Isoude, and grateful to Tristan, on whom he bestowed the honour of chamberlain of the palace, so he had access to the queen at all times.

In the midst of the festivities following the marriage, an unknown minstrel arrived one day, bearing a harp of peculiar construction. He excited King Mark's curiosity by refusing to play on it until he should grant him a boon. The king promised to grant his request and the minstrel, who was none other than Sir Palamedes, the Saracen knight

11. The Queen of Ireland visiting Tristan in his ship.
(Chertsey tile).

and lover of the fair Isoude, sang to the harp a lay in which he demanded Isoude as the promised gift. By the laws of chivalry, King Mark could not withold the boon, and the lady was mounted on her horse and led away by her lover. Needless to say, Tristan was absent at the time. When he returned, he seized his rote and hastened to the shore. Isoude and her new master had already cast off. Tristan played upon his rote and the sound reached the ears of Isoude. She became so deeply moved that Sir Palamedes was induced to return with her to land, that they might see the unknown musician. Tristan waited for his opportunity, seized the lady's horse by the bridle, and made off with her into the forest, tauntingly informing his rival that what he had got by the harp, he had got by the rote. Palamedes took up the pursuit, and a fight was about to begin, when Isoude stepped between them and asked a boon of Palamedes, on the basis of his professed love for her. Palamedes agreed, and Isoude commanded him to leave the contest and go back to Arthur's court, and never to return to her presence. Sir Palamedes burst into tears, saying he would obey her, but beseeching her never to steel her heart against him. She replied that she would remain faithful to her first love, and Palamedes went on his way. Tristan and Isoude remained together in hiding for a week, and then he returned her to her husband, advising him to reward minstrels in some other way in future.

The king made an outward show of gratitude to Tristan, but in his heart he had become bitterly jealous of him. One day, when Tristan and Isoude were alone together in her private chamber, a base and cowardly knight called Andret, spied on them through the keyhole. They were sitting at a chess table, but clearly not attending to the game. Andret went and aroused the king's suspicions, and brought him to look through the keyhole. The king saw enough to confirm his suspicions, and burst into the apartment with his sword drawn. Tristan avoided the first blow, drew his sword and chased the cowardly monarch all over the palace, giving him frequent blows with the flat of his sword. The king cried out for his knights to save him, but none of them dared, nor felt inclined to intervene.

After this affair, Tristan was banished from the kingdom, and Isoude shut up in a tower, which stood on the

**12. Tristan hunting wild beasts in the forest
with his dog named Houdain.**
(Chertsey tile).

bank of a river. Tristan could not bring himself to go into exile without first making some communication with his beloved, so he hid in the forest and contrived to attract her attention by floating curiously-peeled twigs downstream beneath her window. In this way he managed to arrange many secret exchanges. He dwelt in the forest, living on game which Houdain, his faithful dog, ran down for him; he seemed to know his master's wish for concealment, and never barked. At length, Tristan departed, but he left his dog with Isoude as a remembrance of him.

Sir Tristan wandered through many lands, undertaking many brave exploits and achieving glory for himself; yet he remained unhappy because of his separation from his beloved Isoude. It happened, however, that Cornwall was invaded and King Mark was forced to summon his nephew from exile. Tristan obeyed the call, put himself at the head of his uncle's knights, and drove the enemy out of the country. Once more he was in favour and close to his beloved Isoude, but it was only for a time.

Tristan had brought a friend called Pheredin with him, the son of the King of Brittany. When this young knight saw the queen he fell deeply in love with her. Knowing of his friend's love affair with Isoude, Pheredin hid his feelings, but when his health failed him, he wrote and told the queen that he was dying for love of her.

In a moment of pity for Tristan's friend, Isoude sent a kind and passionate letter in reply; so kind that it restored him to health. Unfortunately, Tristan found the letter a few days later, and was taken by the most terrible jealousy. He would have killed Pheredin there and then, had he not made his escape. Then Tristan rode into the forest, where he spent ten days with neither food nor rest*. He was found by a damsel, lying close to death. At first she could not rouse him, but recalling his love of music, she went and brought her harp and played upon it until Tristan came round. His tears flowed, and he breathed more freely; he took the harp and sang the following lay:

> Sweet I sang in former days,
> Kind love perfected in my lays:
> Now my art alone displays
> The woe that on my being preys.

*This may be interpreted as Tristan's descent into hell.

Charming love, delicious power,
Worshipped from my earliest hour,
Thou who life on all dost shower,
Love! my life thou dost devour.

In death's hour I beg of thee,
Isoude, dearest enemy,
Thou who erst could kinder be,
When I'm gone, forget not me.

On my gravestone passers-by,
Oft will read, as low I lie,
"Never wight in love could vie
With Tristan, yet she let him die."

Tristan wrote this lay down and gave it to the damsel, asking her to present it to the queen.

Meanwhile Isoude was inconsolable at Tristan's absence. She discovered it was caused by the fatal letter she had written to Pheredin. She wrote again to the latter, charging him never to see her again. Pheredin obeyed this cruel decree; he went into the forest and died of grief and love in a hermit's cell.

Isoude passed her days in lament over Tristan's absence. One day, when the king entered her chamber unnoticed, he overheard her singing:

Ah, Tristan! far away from me,
Art thou from restless anguish free?
Ah! couldst thou so one moment be,
From her who so much loveth thee?

On hearing these words, the king went into a rage, but Isoude was too far gone to fear him. She confessed her love of Tristan to the king, adding that without doubt he must be dead and that she no longer wished to live.

The king was moved by fair Isoude's distress, and perhaps the idea of Tristan's death had allayed his anger. He told the queen's ladies to take special care of her, and see that she did no harm to herself.

Meanwhile Tristan, although dejected and living more like a savage than a knight, rendered a service to the shepherds by slaying a giant robber who had been plundering their flocks and ransacking their cottages. Out of gratitude, the shepherds carried the hero in triumph to King Mark, with the idea that he would give him a suitable reward. Mark did not recognize the half-naked wild man before him; he ordered him to be well looked after by the queen and her ladies. Needless to say, under such care, Tristan soon recovered and seemed handsomer than ever. Seeing this, King Mark's jealousy revived, and, in spite of his increased debt of gratitude, he again banished him from the court.

Sir Tristan left Cornwall and sought adventures in the land of Leogria (England). One day, when he was travelling through a great forest, he heard the sound of a little bell. He followed the sound and found a hermit who told him that King Arthur had been enticed by a sorceress into that very same forest, and that she had slipped a ring on his finger which had made him forget who or what he was. The sorceress had seduced him and was keeping him there by means of her enchantment. The hermit told him that all the knights of the Round Table were out looking for Arthur, and that he (Tristan) was at the beginning of one of his greatest adventures.

Tristan immediately began the search. He had not gone far before he met Sir Kay, a knight of Arthur's court, who asked where he came from. Tristan told him, and Sir Kay did not miss the opportunity of joking at the expense of a cornish knight. Tristan said nothing, and when they met three other knights, he confirmed Kay's opinion by refusing to joust with them. They all spent the night at an abbey, where Tristan put up with all their jokes about Cornishmen. Kay took the others aside and said that they should leave very early in the morning, so as to be able to surprise the Cornish knight on his way, and have some fun at his expense. Thus, in the morning, Tristan found himself alone; he armed himself and set out to continue his quest. Soon he saw Sir Kay and the others barring his way. They insisted on a joust; Tristan excused himself as long as he could, and then he took his stand. He took them on one after the other, overthrowing all four of them, and then he rode off, bidding them not to forget their friend, the Cornish knight.

He had not ridden far when a damsel cried out, "Oh, my lord, come quickly and prevent a horrid treason!" He flew to her aid, and when he reached the spot he saw a knight, whom three others had borne to the ground, and they were unlacing his helmet in order to cut his head off.

Tristan did not hesitate. He slew one of them with a single stroke of his lance. The knight regained his feet and dispatched another, and the third ran away. The rescued knight raised his visor, and a long white beard fell down over his chest. At once Tristan suspected that it was none other than Arthur himself, and the other knight confirmed his thoughts. Tristan would have knelt before him, but Arthur received him in his arms and asked who he was and where he came from. Tristan declined to tell him, saying he was on a quest which required secrecy. The damsel who had called Tristan to the rescue, had been sent there by the Lady of the Lake, to remove the ring from Arthur's finger and break his enchantment. As soon as she had done so, the sorceress had told the three knights, her brothers, to kill him. King Arthur offered to attach Tristan to his court, where he would reward him with honours. Tristan declined all this, saying he would stay with the king only until he should see him safe with his knights. Soon after, Hector de Marys rode up and saluted the king, who for his part, introduced Tristan as one of the bravest of his knights. Then Tristan took his leave.

He had numerous adventures in which he fulfilled, on all occasions, his duties as a knight, rescuing the oppressed, redressing wrongs, and thus by his constant endeavours relieving the pain of being parted from his loved one. In the meantime, Isoude languished at home; at length, however, unable to wait any longer for news, she wrote a letter to Tristan, and sent it by one of her maids, the niece of the faithful Brengwain. One day, when Tristan was resting by a fountain, the maid arrived there also, and recognized his horse. She perceived his master lying there asleep, woke him and gave him the letter. Tristan derived great pleasure from it, and he begged the maid not to leave until after the magnificent tournament which Arthur had proclaimed, should have taken place. He arranged for her to stay with Persides, a trusty knight who had a castle nearby.

Tristan took Isoude's maid to the tournament, and had her placed on the balcony among the queen's ladies. He then entered the lists, at the height of his strength and valour. Lancelot admired him and, by a secret presentiment, declined to dispute the honour of the day with so gallant a knight. Tristan won the day, and Arthur went down from the balcony to greet the victor, but the modest and devoted Tristan, content with having won in sight of Isoude's messenger, made his escape with her and disappeared.

On the next day of the tournament Tristan assumed different armour as a disguise, but he was soon recognized by the terrible blows that he gave. Arthur had no doubt that it was the same knight. After Lancelot of the Lake and Sir Gawain, Arthur was counted the best knight of the Round Table. He armed himself in secret, in armour which would not give away his identity, and then he went into the tournament. He ran a joust with Tristan, whom he shook in the saddle; but Tristan did not recognize him and threw him off his horse. Arthur got up, content with having tested the stranger knight's strength, and bade Lancelot finish the adventure for the honour of the Round Table. Lancelot assailed Tristan, whose lance was already broken and who was obliged to fight with his sword, using his shield against his opponent's lance. Lancelot's lance pierced Tristan's shield and entered his side, and the tip broke off in the wound. But Tristan struck Lancelot hard on the helmet, cleaving it and wounding him in the head, so that blood flowed into his eyes, momentarily blinding him. Tristan, who thought himself mortally wounded, retired from the field. Lancelot told the king that never in his life had he received such a blow.

Tristan hastened to Gouvernail, his squire, who drew the iron from his wound, and dressed it, giving him immediate ease. Tristan remained in his tent, but Arthur, with the others' consent, decreed him the honours of the second day. Gouvernail, on being questioned, confirmed to them that his master was none other than Tristan of Lionesse, nephew of the King of Cornwall.

King Arthur desired to attach Tristan to his court, and all the knights of the Round Table declared that they could not have a more worthy companion, but Tristan had already slipped away, and Queen Isoude's maid had returned to her mistress.

Sir Tristan rode through a forest and saw ten men fighting, one of them doing battle against the other nine. So he rode up to the knights crying that it was shameful for so many to fight against one. The master of the knights, who was known as Sir Breuse the Pitiless, because of his villainy, warned Tristan not to meddle, and to clear off, for they were not going to let the other knight escape. Tristan replied that it would be a pity for so good a knight to be slain so cowardly, and he warned them that he would help him with all his might.

Then Sir Tristan dismounted, for the others were on foot and he did not wish them to harm his horse. Striking out on the right and the left, he hit a knight with almost every stroke, until they all fled into a tower, shutting Sir Tristan outside. Then he went back to the rescued knight and found him sitting under a tree, sorely wounded. The knight thanked Sir Tristan, who replied by asking him his name. The other answered that he was Sir Palamedes, to which Tristan replied that he hated him more than anyone in the world, and that he must do battle with him. Sir Palamedes pointed out that he had no wish to fight him because of the service he had been rendered, and also that, because of his wounds, he was in no condition to do so. He suggested that Sir Tristan fix another day for the battle, and the latter said they should meet by the river of Camelot, in the meadow where Merlin had set the monument. They went their separate ways, and Sir Tristan went through the forest into a plain, where he rested for six days at a priory.

Then he rode to Camelot, to Merlin's monument, and looked about for Sir Palamedes. He espied a white knight coming towards him, with a covered shield. Tristan welcomed him for having kept his promise, and they came together with all the might of their horses, so fiercely that both knights and horses fell to the ground. Then they got up and began fighting with swords, each one wounding the other sorely so that the grass was red with blood. After four hours fighting thus, without exchanging a word, the white knight spoke, asking the other his name. Tristan was taken aback by the question, asking the other if he were not Sir Palamedes. "No," said the other, "I am Sir Lancelot of the Lake." "Alas!" said Sir Tristan, "what have I done? For you are the man I love best in the world." Then he told Lancelot who he was. They both kneeled down and yielded each other their swords. Then they sat on the stone, took off their helmets, and kissed one another. After a while they rode together towards Camelot, and on the way they met Sir Gawain and Sir Gaheris who had promised Arthur they would not return to his court without bringing Sir Tristan with them.

13. Tristan
(Chertsey tile).

Lancelot told them they could go back, for their quest was accomplished, and he presented them to Sir Tristan. King Arthur came on the scene soon after, and when he knew it was Sir Tristan he said he was as welcome as any knight that ever came to the court. Then Sir Tristan told him of his coming there in search of Sir Palamedes, and of all that had happened. King Arthur took him to the Round Table where he was welcomed by the queen, and many other knights. Arthur welcomed him again as one of the best of knights, the gentlest in the world, a great hunter, and a skilled musician. Then he made Sir Tristan a knight of the Round Table*, taking him to the seat which had previously belonged to Moraunt of Ireland. As he did so, the most melodious sounds were heard, exquisite perfumes filled the air, the name of Moraunt vanished from the seat, and in its place that of Tristan appeared shining forth in light. Tristan's modesty had to be temporarily put aside, for he was obliged by the law of the order to recount all his adventures for the clerks to record in the annals of the Round Table; then he was entitled to take his seat. Lancelot and Guenevere took the occasion to speak to him of fair Isoude, and they expressed the hope that one day a happy chance might bring her to Loegria.

While Tristan was thus honoured at Arthur's court, King Mark's soul was being harassed by malignant jealousy. He could not look upon Isoude without remembering that she loved Tristan, and he set his mind on vengeance. He decided to go disguised into the kingdom of Loegria, and murder Tristan. He took two chosen knights with him, and not wishing to leave Isoude behind, he caused the faithful Brengwain and two other maids to bring her along.

Having arrived near Camelot, Mark divulged his plan to the two knights, who withdrew in horror saying they no longer wished to remain in his service. Mark suspected that his knights would go straight to Arthur, so he had to leave Isoude in an abbey and go on alone to Camelot to refute their accusation.

On his way there, it happened that Mark encountered some of Arthur's knights. The latter recognized him as a

*This is Tristan's second initiation into knighthood; this time he has entered into a spiritually-operative order which can take him beyond the 'lesser mysteries.' Arthur has become his Spiritual Master, and the ups and downs of his previous life can be seen as a preparation for this.

14. King Mark
(Chertsey tile).

Cornish knight, and resolved to have some sport with him. Daguenet, the king's fool, was with them and, although small, he was not without courage. As Mark approached, they armed Daguenet with the idea that he should impersonate Sir Lancelot and challenge the Cornish knight. When King Mark saw an undistinguished-looking knight approaching, he felt no concern, but when the latter called out that he was Sir Lancelot, he panicked and fled, pursued by the shouts and laughter of the other knights.

Meanwhile, at the abbey, Isoude filled in her time by taking occasional walks in the forest. She would stop near a fountain and sing lays to the sound of her harp. One day it happened that Breuse the Pitiless heard her voice. He drew near stealthily, and heard her singing:

Sweet silence, shadowy bower, and verdant lair,
Ye court my troubled spirit to repose,
Whilst I, such dear remembrance rises there,
Awaken every echo with my woes.

Within these woods, by nature's hand arrayed,
A fountain springs, and feeds a thousand flowers;
Ah how my groans do all its murmurs aid!
How my sad eyes do swell it with their showers!

What doth my knight the while? to him is given
A double meed; in love and arms' emprise,
Him the Round Table elevates to heaven*!
Tristan! Ah me! he hears not Isoude's cries.

Breuse the Pitiless, like most other despicable knights, had felt the weight of Tristan's arm, and hated him for it. When he heard this name mentioned by the beautiful songstress, urged by a double impulse he rushed forth and seized his victim. Isoude fainted, and Brengwain filled the air with her shrieks. Breuse carried Isoude to where he had left his horse, but the animal had wandered off and he was obliged to set his burden down whilst he went off in pursuit of it. Just then a knight arrived, drawn by Brengwain's cries; he asked her the cause of her distress. She could not speak, but pointed to her mistress lying in

*This echos the idea that the prime aim of the order of the Round Table was a spiritual one.

a faint on the ground.

By this time, Breuse had returned, and Brengwain's renewed cries told the stranger knight who was the cause of the trouble. The two knights spurred their horses and charged one another; Breuse was thrown, and he lay there pretending to be dead. The stranger knight, who was none other than Tristan, went to attend to the damsels, whilst Breuse mounted his horse and made his escape.

Tristan gently raised Isoude's head and drew aside her golden hair; seeing her face, he gazed upon it for an instant, uttered a cry, and fell back in a swoon. Brengwain came over and soon restored her mistress, and then they turned their attention to the fallen warrior. They raised his visor and discovered he was Tristan. Isoude's tears fell on his face, and their warmth revived him so that he came round in the arms of his beloved.

It was a rule of the Round Table that each new knight should spend ten days on a quest, during which his companions might seek him out in disguised armour and try their strength with him. Tristan had already spent seven days thus, and he had encountered many of the knights of the Round Table and acquitted himself with honour. For the remaining three days of his quest, Isoude remained at the abbey, and then Tristan escorted her to Camelot.

This journey was one of the happiest times in the lives of Tristan and Isoude. He celebrated it in a lay upon a harp:

> With fair Isoude, and with love,
> Ah! how sweet the life I lead!
> How blest forever thus to rove,
> With fair Isoude, and with love!
> As she wills, I live and move,
> And cloudless days to days succeed;
> With fair Isoude, and with love,
> Ah! how sweet the life I lead!
>
> Journeying on from break of day,
> Feel you not fatigued my fair?
> Yon green turf invites to play;
> Journeying on from day to day,
> Ah! let us to that shade away,
> Were it but to slumber there!
> Journeying on from break of day,
> Feel you not fatigued my fair?

77

They arrived at Camelot where they were welcomed by Lancelot, and Isoude was introduced to King Arthur and his queen. King Mark was under arrest because of the Cornish knights' accusation, so Queen Isoude could not rejoin him, and Lancelot placed his castle of La Joyeuse Garde at his friends' disposal.

King Mark found himself obliged either to confess or to clear himself by combat with his accusors. He preferred the former, and King Arthur, as the crime had not been perpetrated, remitted the sentence, only enjoining Mark to lay aside all thoughts of vengeance against his nephew. All parties were formally reconciled before the court; King Mark departed with his queen for Cornwall, whilst Tristan remained at Arthur's court.

During the period when Tristan and Isoude were at La Joyeuse Garde, Sir Tristan rode out one day, without his armour, having no weapon but his spear and sword. He came to a place where he saw two knights in battle, and one of them had overthrown the other. The victor was none other than Sir Palamedes, and when he saw it was Sir Tristan he cried out that now they could settle their old scores. Tristan replied that there never was a Christian who could say he fled from him, and that there would never be a Saracen who could say the same. And there and then Sir Tristan charged Sir Palamedes, and broke his spear upon him. Sir Palamedes saw that Sir Tristan was unarmed and he marvelled at his rashness; however he thought to himself that he would be shamed if he were to slay Sir Tristan without his armour, and he held back. Then Sir Tristan called him a coward, but Sir Palamedes replied by asking Sir Tristan what he would do if he were well armed and himself unarmed. Sir Tristan understood, and then he asked Sir Palamedes why he would not be christened. Sir Palamedes replied that it was because of a vow that he had made many years ago, and that he had one more battle to fight before he would be christened. Then Sir Tristan told him he need not wait long, for he would take the armour of the fallen knight, and then they could fight on equal terms. Tristan went across to the defeated knight and asked him to lend him his armour. Sir Galleron, for that was the name of the knight, agreed, and Tristan armed himself, mounted his horse, and he and Sir Palamedes did battle. Sir Palamedes broke his spear on Tristan's shield, and then they dismounted and fought with swords for more than two hours. Tristan was the first to be wounded, but then he wounded Sir Palamedes in the shoulder, and at the same time struck his sword from his hand. Sir Palamedes was helpless, but Sir Tristan offered to let him pick up his sword. Sir Palamedes, for his part, replied that he had no wish to fight the battle any more; he pointed out that his only offence had been his love of fair Isoude; he begged Tristan to forgive him, and added that now he could go to a church to be christened and they could both return to Camelot for the feast of Pentecost. This they did, and when they arrived at Camelot all the court were glad at the news.

Soon after these events, but after Isoude had returned to Cornwall, Sir Gawain returned to Arthur's court with the news from Merlin that it was time to begin the quest of the Holy Grail. Tristan determined to enter upon the quest, and he immediately set out for Brittany where he hoped to obtain counsel as to the best course to pursue. On arriving in Brittany, he found King Hoel engaged in a war with a rebellious vassal, and hard pressed by his enemy. He had lost many of his best knights, and did not know where to turn for aid. Tristan volunteered to help; Hoel placed him at the head of his armed men who were so inspired by his example and leadership that they gained a complete victory. Full of gratitude, the king offered his daughter to Tristan. The princess was beautiful and accomplished, and bore the same name as the Queen of Cornwall; so they called her Isoude of the White Hands to distinguish her from Isoude the Fair.

Tristan was torn by internal conflict. He adored the first Isoude, but his love for her was hopeless and not unaccompanied by remorse. Moreover, the sacred quest on which he had now entered demanded of him perfect purity of life. It seemed as if destiny had provided the charming Princess Isoude of the White Hands as the best security for his good resolutions. This last thought determined him. They were married, and passed some months in tranquil happiness at the court of King Hoel. The pleasure which Tristan felt in his wife's society increased day by day. An inward grace had seemed to stir within him from the moment when he had taken the oath to go on the quest of the Holy Grail; it seemed even to have triumphed over the power of the magic love-potion.

The war broke out again, and once more Tristan played

a leading role. The enemy was eventually obliged to retreat and shut himself up in his principal city. Tristan led the attack, but as he attempted to scale the walls, he was struck on the head by a rock thrown from above. He fell to the ground, where he lay unconscious.

As soon as he came round, he asked to be carried back to his wife. The princess was skilled in the art of surgery and she insisted that she alone should attend to his wound. She bandaged his head with her fair hands, and Tristan kissed them with gratitude, which began to grow into love. At first, Isoude's devoted care seemed to have a beneficial effect, but after a while, despite all her care, the malady began to grow worse, day by day.

Tristan's old squire reminded him that the Princess of Ireland, now Queen of Cornwall, had once cured him under similar discouraging circumstances. Tristan called Isoude of the White Hands and told her of his former cure. He added that he believed she could cure him and that she would surely come if sent for.

Isoude of the White Hands sent Gesnes, a trusty man and skilled navigator, to Cornwall. Before he set sail, Tristan gave him a ring to present to the Queen of Cornwall and told him to tell her that he was near to death and in need of her aid. He further told Gesnes that if he succeeded in bringing her, he should hoist white sails on his ship as he returned; if she refused to come, he should hoist black sails which would be the presage of his impending death.

Gesnes performed his mission successfully. King Mark happened to be absent from his capital, and the queen readily consented to return with him to Brittany. Gesnes clothed the vessel in the whitest of sails, and sped back across the sea.

Meanwhile, Tristan's wound steadily worsened. He was no longer well enough to be carried to the seaside daily, as had been his custom from the first day he thought the ship might be returning from Cornwall. He gave a young damsel the task of keeping watch over the sea, and to come and tell him the colour of the sails when she saw a vessel approaching from the direction of Cornwall.

When Isoude of the White Hands had consented to send for the Queen of Cornwall, she had no knowledge of the effect this might have on her own happiness. Now that she had learnt more, she thought it prudent to keep all

15. Isoude and Brengwain approaching the
coast of Brittany
(Chertsey tile).

knowledge of the queen's arrival from her husband, with the idea of employing her medical skill through an intermediary. In this way she hoped to avert the dangers of renewed personal contact between the two. When the ship was seen approoaching, with its white sails sparkling in the sun, the damsel, by command of her mistress, carried word to Tristan that the sails were black.

Tristan, overcome with inexpressible grief, breathed a profound sigh, turned his face away, and said: "Alas, my beloved, we shall never see one another again!" Then he commended himself to God, and breathed his last.

News of Tristan's death was the first thing the Queen of Cornwall heard on landing. She was taken almost senseless to his chamber, where she expired holding him in her arms.

Before he died, Tristan had requested that his body be sent to Cornwall, and that his sword, with a letter he had written, should be delivered to King Mark. The bodies of Tristan and Isoude were sent to Cornwall, along with the sword and letter, which were presented to the king. Mark was melted with tenderness when he saw the weapon which slew Moraunt of Ireland, a weapon which had so often saved his life and redeemed his kingdom. In the letter Tristan asked forgiveness of his uncle and told him about the love-potion.

Mark ordered the lovers to be buried in his own chapel. From Tristan's tomb there sprung a vine, which went along the walls, and descended into the queen's grave. It was cut down three times, but each time it sprung up again with greater vigour, and this wonderful plant has ever since shaded the tombs of Tristan and Isoude.

CHAPTER 7. SEEKING THE PRINCESS

Celtic literature abounds in tales based on the world-wide theme of the quest of the princess. Often the hero is a knight, a member of the warrior class, but in some of Luzel's Breton tales he is an artizan, tradesman, or peasant-farmer. Sometimes the hero begins the quest voluntarily, after hearing of the beauty, or plight of the princess; in other cases the hero is sent on the quest by someone with power or authority over him, implying destiny rather than free will. The princess is usually situated in a far-off castle, which can only be reached by a difficult and hazardous journey. Sometimes her father is introduced simply as a king, but often he is a magician-king. In a few versions the princess is held prisoner by a wicked magician who has usurped the the true king and subverted the kingdom. The boundary of the magician, or the magician-king's domain is generally represented by a vast expanse of water, a desert*, or a great forest. This boundary marks the entrance to the 'other world' of the 'lower waters' or world of the psyche. These tales can often be explained in terms of microcosmic, or interior symbolism: The princess represents the Spirit within, and the magician, man's internal anti-spiritual tendences and forces. This type of quest tale is therefore generally symbolic of the lesser mysteries, the journey across the psychic realm of the 'other world.' Marriage to the princess represents marriage to the Spirit (in the sense of the outside of the heart) and the return to the primordial state of True Man.

In some of these tales, the hero has to kill the old king or magician before he can marry the princess; in others, the old king dies afterwards, for example, from eating too much at the wedding feast, or by simply fading away. The death of the old king can be understood in two senses, one historical, and the other symbolic:

The historical interpretation takes us back to very ancient times: In the pre-Indo-European settled traditions of the Mediterranean region, the female principle identified with the Supreme Diety. The Earth Mother was 'she who is all that is, that was, or ever shall be, the eternal giver of life.' The male principle was the fecund power that impregnated the fertile universe, but which in itself

*In these old tales a desert implies a wilderness or uninhabited place.

was susceptible to decay and loss of power. Thus in those ancient times, the yearly king, after having impregnated the queen, was killed and ploughed back into the land to fertilize it. This idea persisted even after these old societies had been overrun by Indo-Europeans with their Sky-Gods, but the Mother Goddess was then relegated to a subsidiary position in the pantheon and the king was rejuvenated by a special ceremony which avoided his sacrifice and replacement. The idea that the king must die in many of the Celtic princess-quest tales may well, therefore, indicate their great antiquity.

From the point of view of interior symbolism, however, the death of the old king or magician in many of these tales implies the death of the ego, or self, prior to rebirth as True Man. In these cases, the old king symbolises an inferior part of the hero himself.

As an example of this type of quest tale, we give the story of Culhwch and Olwen from the Mabinogion:

Culhwch and Olwen.

Culydd, the son of prince Celyddon, chose as his wife Goleudid, the daughter of prince Anlawd. When they were married, the people prayed that they might have an heir, and they had a son whom they called Culhwch.

After this the boy's mother, Goleudid, the daughter of prince Anlawd, fell sick. She called her husband to her, telling him that she was going to die of her illness, and that he would wish to take another wife. She reminded him that it would be wrong to harm his son by marrying someone who would be jealous of him. With this in mind, she charged him not to take a wife until he saw a briar with two blossoms growing on her grave, and this he promised her. Then she asked him to see that her grave would be tended every year, so that no weeds might grow upon it. Then she died. The king did as she had requested, and every morning he sent an attendant to see if anything were growing on the grave. At the end of the seventh year, however, they neglected the grave.

One day the king went out hunting, and he rode to the burial place, to see the grave, and to know if it were time that he should take a wife; and the king saw the briar. Then he took counsel where he should find a wife, and one of his counsellors advised him to take the wife of

84

King Doged. And Culydd set out and conquered his lands, slaying him and marrying his widow, who was the sister of Ysbaddaden Penkawr.

One day his stepmother said to Culhwch that he should take a wife. Culhwch replied that he was not old enough to marry. And then she declared to him that his destiny was not to wed until he could obtain Olwen, the daughter of Ysbaddaden Penkawr, to be his wife. At the mention of the name of Olwen, the youth blushed, and love for her diffused throughout his frame, so that his father asked him what had come over him. He told his father of his stepmother saying he would never have a wife until he obtained Olwen, the daughter of Ysbaddaden Penkawr. His father told him that it should not be difficult for him as a cousin of King Arthur. He told him to go, therefore, to Arthur and ask him to cut his hair and grant him a boon.

And the youth went forth on a steed with head dappled gray, four winters old, firm of limb, with shell-formed hoofs, having a bridle of linked gold on his head, and a saddle of costly gold. And in the youth's hand were two spears of silver, sharp, well-tempered, headed with steel, three ells in length, of an edge to wound the wind and cause blood to flow, and swifter than the fall of the dew-drop from the blade of reed-grass, when the dew of June is at the heaviest. A gold-hilted sword was at his thigh, the blade of which was gilded, bearing a cross of inlaid gold of the hue of the lightning of heaven. His war-horn was of ivory. Before him were two brindled, white-breasted greyhounds, having strong collars of rubies about their necks, reaching from the shoulder to the ear. And the one that was on the left side bounded across to the right side, and the one on the right to the left, and, like two sea-swallows sported around him... And the blade of grass bent not beneath him, so light was his courser's tread, as he journeyed towards the gate of Arthur's palace.

The youth called out: "Is there a porter?" "There is; and if you don't keep your peace, small will be your welcome. I am Arthur's porter every first day of January." "Open the gate." "I will not open it." "Why not?" "The knife is in the meat, and the drink is in the horn, and there is revelry in Arthur's hall; and none may enter therein but the son of a king of a priviliged country, or a craftsman bringing his craft. But there will be refreshment for your dogs as well as your horse; and for you there will be collops cooked and peppered, and the best of wine, and mirthful songs; and food for fifty men shall be brought to you in the guest-chamber, where the stranger and the sons of other countries eat, who come not into the precincts of Arthur's palace. You shall fare no worse there than if you were with Arthur in the court. A lady shall smooth your couch and lull you with songs; and early tomorrow morning, when the gate is open, you shall be the first to go in and choose your place in Arthur's hall." But the youth said: "That I will not do. If you open the gate, all right. If not, I will bring disgrace upon your lord and evil report upon you. And I will make three great shouts at this gate which will prove deadlier than any ever heard here." "Whatever clamour you may care to make, you shall not enter against the laws of the palace, at least not until I have spoken with Arthur," said the porter.

Then the porter went into the hall, and Arthur said to him: "Have you news from the gate?" "Half of my life is passed," said the porter, "and half of yours, and I have travelled in many lands, but never have I seen a man of equal dignity to the one now outside the gate." And then Arthur said: "If you came here walking, go back running, for it is unbecoming to keep a man such as you describe, out in the wind and rain." But Kay said: "If you would follow my advice, you would not break the laws of the court because of him." "Not so," said Arthur; "it is an honour to us to be resorted to, and the greater our courtesy, the greater will be our renown and our fame and our glory."

And the porter went to the gate and opened it wide for Culhwch; and although all dismounted on the horse-block at the gate, yet he did not do so, but rode into the hall upon his charger. Then he said: "Greetings to the ruler of this island, and may this greeting be no less unto the lowest than the highest, and equally to your guests and your warriors and chieftains; let all partake of it as completely as yourself. And may your favour, your fame, and your glory be complete throughout this island." Arthur greeted him in return, and said: "Sit between two of my warriors, and you shall have minstrels before you, and, as long as you remain here, you shall enjoy the priveleges of a king born to a throne. And when I dispense gifts to my visitors, you shall be the first to receive." But the youth said: "I did not come here to consume meat and drink; but if I obtain the boon that I seek, I shall praise you everywhere;

16. Porter at the gate
(Chertsey tile).

if not, I shall shame you to the four quarters of the earth, everywhere your fame has spread." Then Arthur said: "If you will not stay here, you shall have whatever boon you may name, except for my ship, my sword and lance, and Guenevere, my wife. By heaven you shall have it cheerfully, name what you will." "First bless my hair," said he.

And Arthur took a golden comb, and scissors with loops of silver, and he combed his hair. And Arthur asked him who he was; "for my heart warms to you, and I know you are of my blood." The youth replied: "I am Culhwch, the son of Culydd, the son of Prince Celyddon, by Goleudid my mother, the daughter of Prince Anlawd." "That is true," said Arthur; "you are my cousin, and whatever boon you may ask, you shall receive." "The boon I ask is that you obtain for me Olwen, the daughter of Ysbaddaden Penkawr, to be my wife; and this boon I likewise seek at the hands of your warriors." And he asked for the boon in the name of many of Arthur's warriors, and other famous persons.

Then Arthur said: "I have never heard of the maiden of whom you speak, nor of her kindred, but I will gladly send messengers in search of her, if you will give me time." "I willingly grant you from now until the end of the year," said the youth. Then Arthur sent messengers to every land in his dominions, but at the end of the year, Arthur's messengers returned without having learnt anything about Olwen. Then Culhwch said: "Everyone has received his boon, except for me. I will leave and take your honour away with me." Then Kay said: "Rash Chieftain! Are you reproaching Arthur? Come with us, and we will not part until either you confess the maiden does not exist, or we find her." Thereupon Kay rose up, and Arthur called for Bedwyr, who never shrank from any enterprise upon which Kay was bound. None were equal to him in swiftness except Arthur himself; and although he was one-handed, he could shed blood on the field of battle faster than three warriors.

And Arthur called to Cyndelig, the guide, enjoining him also to go on the expedition, for he was as good a guide in a strange land as in his own.

He called Gurhyr Gwalstat, because he knew all tongues.

He called Gawain, the son of Gwyar, because he never returned home without having achieved his quest.

And Arthur called Meneu in order that, if they went into

a savage country, he might cast a charm and an illusion over them, so that they might see without being seen.

They journeyed until they came to a vast open plain, where they saw a great castle; the fairest in the world. And when they came near the castle, they saw a vast flock of sheep. There was a herdsman on a mound nearby and he was clothed in skins; by his side was a shaggy mastiff, bigger than a horse.

Kay told Gurhyr to go and salute the shepherd, but he replied that he had not engaged to go alone in advance, so they agreed to go there together. Meneu told them to have no fear, for he would cast a spell upon the giant dog so that he would injure no one. And they went up to the herdsman and asked him whose sheep he kept, and who was the owner of the castle. The herdsman told them they must be stupid not to know that it was the castle of Ysbaddaden Penkawr. In his turn, the herdsman asked who they were. They replied, informing him that they were an embassy from Arthur, come to seek Olwen, the daughter of Ysbaddaden Penkawr. The herdsman replied: "Heaven's mercy be upon you, for none who ever came on this quest has ever returned alive." And the herdsman got up to go, and Culhwch gave him a ring of gold. And he went home and showed the ring to his wife, saying that those who had given it would be seeing them in the evening. His wife asked who they were; when she heard that Culhwch was among them, she felt happy that her sister's son was coming to see her; but she was also sad when she learnt that he was coming to seek Olwen, for she had never seen anyone return alive from that quest.

Like the herdsman and his dog, his wife was also of gigantic proportions. When they came in the evening, she rushed out to embrace them, but Kay took a log from the fire and placed it between her hands; she squeezed it so that it became all twisted, and he said that if she had squeezed him thus, it would have been an evil welcome. They went into the house and ate. Soon after, the woman opened a chest and out came a youth with curly yellow hair. He was the last of her sons; the others, all twenty-three of them, had been killed by Ysbaddaden Penkawr. Kay asked her to let her son go with him, saying that he would not be killed unless he also was killed with him. Then she tried to dissuade them from the quest, but they would not be put off. They asked if they might see Olwen, and she told them that she came there every Saturday to wash her hair, and that she always left her rings behind in the vessel, and never sent anyone to fetch them. Then they asked if she would come if she were sent for, and the woman said she would only send for her if they promised not to harm her. This they did; so a message was sent, and she came.

She was clothed in a robe of flame-coloured silk, and about her neck was a collar of ruddy gold, on which were precious emeralds and rubies. More yellow was her head than the flower of the broom, and her skin was whiter than the foam of the wave, and fairer were her hands and her fingers than the blossoms of the wood-anemone amidst the spray of the meadow fountain. The eye of the trained hawk was not brighter than hers. Her bosom was more snowy than the breast of the white swan, her cheek redder than the reddest roses. Whoever saw her was filled with her love. Four white trefoils sprung up wherever she trod, and that is why they called her Olwen.

She came into the house and sat on the front bench, next to Culhwch; and as soon as he saw her, he knew her. He told her that he had loved her for many a day; and he asked her to go away with him. She explained that she could not do so, for she had promised her father that she would not go without his approval, for his life would only last until the time of her marriage*. She therefore advised him to go to her father and grant whatever he asked, and that in doing so he would obtain his desire. She added a warning that if he denied her father anything, he would be lucky to escape with his life. Culhwch promised that he would try, should the occasion present itself.

She returned to the castle, and they all followed behind her. They slew the nine porters who were at the nine gates, in silence. And they slew the nine watch-dogs without one of them barking. And they went forward to the hall.

They greeted Ysbaddaden Penkawr, and he, in return

*In this story, Culhwch represents that part of a man's soul which longs for the Spirit. Olwen represents the Spirit within. The great plain with the castle in it should be seen as the psychic 'other world.' Ysbaddaden Penkawr means 'Hawthorn, Chief of the Giants;' He symbolises the base self, prickly and monstrous, which must die before spiritual rebirth, represented by marriage to Olwen, can take place.

asked them why they had come. "We come to ask for your daughter Olwen, for Culhwch, the son of Culydd, the son of Prince Celyddon," they said. "Where are my pages and my servants? Raise up the forks beneath my two eyebrows, which have fallen over my eyes, so I may see the quality of my son-in-law." And they did so. "Come back tomorrow, and you shall have an answer," he said.

As they were leaving, Ysbaddaden Penkawr seized one of the three poisoned darts that lay beside him and threw it at them; but Bedwyr caught it and flung it back, and it wounded Ysbaddaden Penkawr in the knee. Then he said: "A cursed ungentle son-in-law, truly! I shall ever walk the worse for this rudeness and shall ever be without a cure. This poisoned iron pains me like the bite of a gad-fly. Cursed be the smith who forged it, and the anvil on which it was wrought! So sharp is it!"

They spent the night in the herdsman's house. The next day they went again to the castle and said to Ysbaddaden Penkawr: "Give us your daughter in consideration of her dowry and her maiden fee, which we will pay to you and to her two kinswomen likewise." Then he said: "Her grandmothers and her four great-grandfathers are still alive; I must ask their advice." "Do so," they answered, and as they were about to leave, he took the second dart and threw it at them. And Meneu caught it and flung it back at him, and wounded him in the middle of the chest. "A cursed ungentle son-in-law, truly!" said he; "the hard iron pains me like the bite of a horse-leech. Cursed be the hearth whereon it was heated and the smith who formed it. So sharp is it! Henceforth, whenever I go uphill, I shall have scant breath and a pain in my chest, and I shall often loathe my food." And they left and went to meat.

And the third day they returned to the castle. And Ysbaddaden Penkawr said to them: "Shoot not at me again unless you desire death. Where are my attendants? Lift up the forks of my eyebrows, which have fallen over my eyeballs, that I may see the quality of my son-in-law." Then they arose, and as they did so, he took a third dart and threw it at them. And Culhwch caught it, and threw it vigorously back and wounded him in the eyeball. "A cursed ungentle son-in-law, truly! As long as I remain alive, my eyesight will be the worse. Whenever I go against the wind, my eyes will water; and perhaps my head will burn, and I shall have a giddiness every new moon. Like the bite of a mad dog is the stroke of this poisoned iron. Cursed be the fire in which it was forged!" And they left and went to meat.

And the next day they came again to the castle, and said: "Shoot not at us any more, unless you wish even more hurt, harm, and torture than you have already." Culhwch said: "Give me your daughter; if you will not, you shall die because of her." "Where is he that seeks my daughter? Come closer, where I may see you." And they placed him in a chair face-to-face with him.

Ysbaddaden Penkawr asked him if he were the one who sought his daughter, and Culhwch replied: "It is I."

"I must have your pledge that you will treat me justly; and when I have obtained what I ask for, you shall have my daughter."

"I promise you that, willingly," said Culhwch; "name what you will."

"I will do so," he said. "Do you see that red-tilled earth over there?"

"I see it."

"When I first met the mother of this maid, nine bushels of flax were sown there, and none has yet sprung up, white nor black. I require you to have the flax to sow in the new land over there, so that when it grows up it may make a white whimple for my daughter's head on your wedding day."

"It will be easy for me to do this, although you may think otherwise."

"Though you may get this, there remains what you will not get; Teirtu's harp, to play to us that night. When a man desires it to play, it does so by itself; and when he desires it to stop, it stops. And Teirtu will not give it up of his own free will, and you will not be able to compel him."

"It will be easy for me to do this, although you may think otherwise."

"Though you may obtain this, there is that which you will not obtain. I require you to get me Mabon, the son of Modron, to be my huntsman. He was taken from his mother when three nights old, and it is not known where he is, or whether he is alive or dead."

"It will be easy for me to do this, though you may think otherwise."

"Though you may get this, there is still that which you

may not get; the two cubs of the wolf Gast Rhymhi; no leash in the world will hold them, except a leash made from the beard of Dillus Varwawe, the robber. And the leash will be of no use unless plucked from his beard while he is alive. While he lives, he will not allow anyone to do this to him, and should he be dead, the leash will be too brittle for use."

"It will be easy for me to do this, though you may not think it so."

"Though you obtain this, there is yet that which you will not obtain; the sword of Gwernach the Giant; he will not give it of his own free will, and you will never be able to compel him."

"It will be easy for me to do this, though you may not think it so."

"Though you get this, you shall never get all of these things. In seeking them you shall meet with difficulties, and spend sleepless nights, and if you do not obtain them all, you shall not have my daughter."

"I shall have horses, and knights; and my lord and kinsman, Arthur, will obtain all these things for me. And I shall gain your daughter, and you shall lose your life."

"Go forward, and you shall not be charged for food and clothing for my daughter whilst you are seeking these things; and when you have accomplished all these marvels, you shall have my daughter to be your wife."

They set out, and journeyed all day until they came to a vast castle, the largest in the world. And a black man, bigger than any three men of this world, came out from the castle. And they said to him: "Oh man, whose castle is it?" "You must be stupid, for everyone in the world knows this is the castle of Gwernach the Giant." "What welcome awaits guests and strangers who go there?" "Oh, Chieftain, Heaven protect you! No guest ever came back from there alive, and no one may enter, unless he brings his craft."

Then they went towards the gate. Gurhyr Gwalstat said: "Is there a porter?" "There is; why do you ask?" "Open the gate." "I will not open it." "Why not?" "The knife is in the meat, and the drink is in the horn, and there is revelry in the hall of Gwernach the Giant; and except for a craftsman who brings his craft, the gate will not be opened to-night." "Truly, porter," said Kay, "I bring my craft with me." "What is your craft?" "Burnishing swords;

I am the best in the world." "I will go and tell Gwernach the Giant of this, and I will bring you an answer."

So the porter went in, and Gwernach asked him if he had news from the gate. He told him that there was a party at the gate, one of whom was skilled at burnishing swords. Gwernach said that he had been seeking someone to polish his sword, and he told the porter to let the man enter who was bringing his craft.

The porter went back and opened the gate. And Kay went in by himself, and he saluted Gwernach the Giant. And a chair was placed for him opposite Gwernach. And Gwernach said to him: "Is it true, what I have been told, that you know how to burnish swords?" "I know full well how to do so," answered Kay. Then Gwernach's sword was brought to him, and Kay took a blue whetstone from beneath his arm, and asked whether he wanted it burnished white or blue. "Do what seems best; as you would if it were your own." Then Kay polished one half of the blade and put it in his hand. "How do you like this?" he asked. "I would rather that the whole of it were like this, than all that is in my dominions. It is a marvel to me that a man such as you should have no companion." "Oh, noble sir, I have a companion, but he is not skilled in this art." "Who is he?" "Send the porter for him; he will know him because the head of his lance will leave its shaft, draw blood from the wind, and return to its place again." Then the gate was opened, and Bedwyr came in, and Kay said: "Bedwyr is very skilful, though he does not know this art."

And there was much talking amongst those outside, because Kay and Bedwyr had got in. The herdsman's only son was with them, and he got in also; and he managed to let the others in, but they kept themselves concealed.

The sword was now polished, and Kay handed it to the giant, to see if he were pleased with the work. And the giant said: "The work is good, and I am pleased with it." Then Kay said: "It is your scabbard which has rusted your sword; give it to me so that I may take out the wooden sides of it, and put in new ones." And he took the scabbard from him, and the sword in the other hand. And he came and stood next to the giant, making as though to put the sword into the scabbard; but with it he struck at the giant's neck, and cut off his head at one blow. Then they despoiled the castle, taking what goods and jewels they would. And they returned to Arthur's court, bringing with them the sword of Gwernach the Giant.

And when they told Arthur how they had fared, Arthur said: "It is a good beginning." Then they took counsel, and said: "Which of these marvels will it be best for us to seek next?" "It will be best," said one, "to seek Mabon, the son of Modron; and he will not be found unless first we find Eidoel, the son of Aer, his kinsman." Then they rose up, Arthur and his warriors, to seek Eidoel; and they journeyed until they came to the castle of Glivi, where Eidoel was imprisoned. Glivi stood on the summit of his castle, and he said: "Arthur, what do you want of me, for I have nothing left in this fortress, and I have neither joy nor pleasure in it, nor wheat nor oats? Therefore, seek not to harm me." And Arthur replied: "I did not come here to harm you, but to seek your prisoner." "I will give you my prisoner, though I had not thought to give him up to anyone, and that shall be my support for you."

Arthur's followers said to him: "Lord, go home, for you cannot proceed with your host in quest of such small adventures as these." Then Arthur said: "It is good that you, Gurhyr Gwalstat, are going on this quest, for you know all languages, and are familiar with those of the birds and the beasts*. You, Eidoel, should likewise go in search of your cousin. And as for you, Kay and Bedwyr, I have high hopes that you will achieve whatever adventures you may seek. You should achieve this adventure for me."

They went on until they came to the Ousel of Cilgwri. And Gurhyr adjured her, saying: "Tell me if you know anything of Mabon, the son of Modron, who was taken when three nights old from between his mother and the wall." And the Ousel answered: "When I first came here, there was a smith's anvil in this place, and I was then a young bird; and from that time no work has been done upon it except the pecking of my beak every evening; and now there is not so much as the size of a nut left of it; yet during all this time, I have never heard of the man for whom you inquire. However, I will do what is right for an embassy from Arthur. There is a race of animals who were formed before me, and I will be your guide to them."

So they went to the place of the Stag of Redynvre, and

*A probable reference to Shamanism. This, together with the earlier reference to the magical powers of Meneu, implies that this Arthurian tale goes back to the pre-Christian, Pagan time of the Shaman-Druids.

they said: "Stag of Redynvre, we are an embassy from Arthur, and we have come because we have not heard of any animal older than you. Do you know anything about Mabon, the son of Modron, who was taken from his mother when three nights old?" The Stag said: "When I first came here there was a plain all around me, without any trees save one oak sapling, which grew up to be an oak with a hundred branches; and that oak has since perished, so that nothing remains of it but its withered stump; and from that day to this I have been here, yet never have I heard of the man for whom you inquire. Nevertheless, as you are an embassy from Arthur, I will be your guide to the place where there is an animal which was formed before I was, and the oldest animal in the world, and the one that has travelled most, the Eagle of Gwern Abwy."

Gurhyr said: "Eagle of Gwern Abwy, we have come to you, an embassy from Arthur, to ask if you know anything of Mabon, the son of Modron, who was taken from his mother when three nights old?" The Eagle said: "I have been here for a great space of time, and when I first came, there was a rock from the top of which I pecked at the stars every evening; and it has crumbled away, and now it is not so much as a span high. All that time I have been here, and I have never heard of the man for whom you inquire, except once when I went in search of food as far as Llyn Llyw. And whilst I was there, I stuck my talons into a salmon, thinking he would serve me as food for a long time. But he drew me into the water, and I was lucky to escape from him. After that I made peace with him, and I drew fifty fish-spears out of his back and relieved him. Unless he knows something of him whom you seek, I cannot say who may. Anyway, I will guide you to the place where he is."

So they went there, and the Eagle said: "Salmon of Llyn Llyw, I have come to you with an embassy from Arthur, to ask if you know anything of Mabon, the son of Modron*, who was taken away at three nights old from his mother?" "I will tell you as much as I know. With every tide I go along the river upstream, until I come near the walls of Gloucester, and there have I found such

---

*The frequent repetition of lines may indicate that this tale comes from ancient, oral tradition; such repetition gave the storyteller time to remember what came next.

a wrong as I never found elsewhere; and to be sure that you will believe me, let two of you go there, one on each of my shoulders." So Kay and Gurhyr Gwalstat went upon the salmon's shoulders, and they swam until they reached the wall of the prison; and they heard a great wailing and lamenting from the dungeon. Gurhyr said: "Who is it that laments in this house of stone?" "Alas! It is Mabon, the son of Modron, who is here imprisoned; and no imprisonment was ever so grievous as mine." "Have you hope of being released for gold or silver, or for any gifts of wealth, or through battle and fighting?" "By fighting will whatever I may gain be obtained."

And they returned to Arthur, and told him where Mabon, the son of Modron, was imprisoned. And Arthur* summoned the warriors of the island, and they journeyed as far as Gloucester, to the place where Mabon was in prison. Kay and Bedwyr went upon the shoulders of the fish, whilst Arthur's warriors attacked the castle. And during all the fighting, Kay broke through the wall into the dungeon and brought away the prisoner upon his back. And Arthur returned home, and Mabon at liberty, with him.

On a certain day as Gurhyr Gwalstat was walking over a mountain, he heard a wailing and a grievous cry. And when he heard it, he sprung forward and went towards it. And when he came there, he saw a fire burning among the turf, and an ant-hill nearly surrounded by the fire. And he drew his sword and smote off the ant-hill close to the

*In this later part of the story, Culhwch has faded into the background, and Arthur and his warriors play a leading role. Ysbaddaden Penkawr has set Culhwch a series of seemingly impossible tasks. Culhwch can only succeed with the help of Arthur (his Spiritual Master) nd Arthur's warriors (spiritual forces invoked or called into play by Arthur). These forces symbolised by Arthur's warriors may be seen both as aids from 'above,' and as elements within Culhwch's soul. The impossible tasks may be likened to the insurmountable obstacles which seem to separate man from the Spirit. When man persists in the spiritual quest, his methods may seem totally inadequate to deal with these obstacles; through his perseverance, however, they disappear, for they were never there. Once these illusions have gone, the Spirit alone remains to shine forth. This story may also have a literal interpretation, but since it tells us of adventures in the 'other world' it must be understood as experienced in a trance, or similar state. Any such literal interpretation does not, of course, invalidate the foregoing comments.

17. Illustrations to Culhwch and Olwen
(from Lady Guest's Mabinogion, 1877).

98

ground, so that it escaped being burned in the fire. And the ants said to him: "Receive from us Heaven's blessing, and that which no man can give, we will give you." Then they fetched the nine bushels of flax-seed which Ysbaddaden Penkawr had required of Culhwch, and they brought the full measure, without lacking any, except one flax-seed, and that a lame ant brought in before nightfall.

Then Arthur said: "Which of the marvels will it be best to seek next?" "It will be best to seek the two cubs of the wolf Gast Rhymhi."

"Is it known where she is?" asked Arthur. "She is in Aber Cleddyf," said one. Then Arthur went to Tringad's house, in Aber Cleddyf, and he asked him whether he had heard of her there. He replied: "She has often slain my herds, and she is down there in a cave."

Then Arthur went in his ship Prydwen by sea, and the others went by land to hunt her. And they surrounded her and her two cubs, and took them and carried them away.

As Kay and Bedwyr sat on a beacon-cairn on the summit of Plynlimon, in the highest wind that ever was, they looked around them and saw a great smoke, afar off. Then Kay said: "By the hand of my friend, there is the fire of a robber." Then they hurried towards the smoke, and when they were near they could see Dillus Varwawe scorching a wild boar. "Behold the greatest robber who ever fled from Arthur," said Bedwyr to Kay. "Then you know him?" "Yes I do; he is Dillus Varwawe, and no leash in the world will be able to hold the cubs of the Gast Rhymhi, except one made from his beard. And even that will be useless unless plucked out alive, with wooden tweezers; for if dead it will be brittle." "What should we do?" asked Bedwyr. "Let us leave him to eat his fill," said Kay, "and after that he will fall asleep." And whilst they waited, they employed themselves in making wooden tweezers. And when Kay was sure he was asleep, he dug a pit beneath his feet, struck him a violent blow, and squeezed him into the pit. And then they twitched out his beard completely with the wooden tweezers, and after that they killed him. And they made a leash from the beard, and took it to Arthur.

Thus they obtained all the marvels that Ysbaddaden Penkawr had required of Culhwch; and they all set out to his court. And Culhwch said to Ysbaddaden Penkawr: "Is your daughter mine now?" "She is yours," he said, "but you have no need to thank me, but Arthur, who has accomplished this for you." Then the herdsman's son, whose brothers had been slain by Ysbaddaden Penkawr, seized him by the hair, dragged him to the keep, and cut off his head. Then they took possession of the castle and all its treasures. And that night Olwen became Culhwch's bride, and she remained his wife as long as she lived.

CHAPTER 8. THE QUEST OF THE HOLY GRAIL.

Before looking into the symbolism of the Quest of the Holy Grail, we think it right to say a few words about Arthur and the Arthurian legends. No doubt Arthur was great in the temporal and military sense, in that he led a successful military campaign which checked the advance of the Saxons for a significant period. In temporal terms, however, he was at first probably little more than a chieftain or prince of the Silures in South Wales. At the time of his great victories, however, he seems to have figured as the Commander-in-Chief of the united British resistance. His real greatness, and right to the title of True King, must come from his spiritual rank. Some writers have derived his name from the old Celtic deity *Artaius*, or from *Arcturus*, the Great Bear; others have linked it with the Latin *arthros*, meaning a joint. The implication of the latter is 'he who joins Heaven and Earth*;' the spiritual 'pole'. No doubt the historical evidence for Arthur is scant, but this is true of many who have been great in spheres neither temporal nor military. The historical evidence for Shakespeare, for example, is so slight that some historians have doubted if he ever wrote or even existed, and yet we have the great works bearing his name. Likewise the contemporary historians of Jesus noticed him so little that only one of them, Josephus, mentioned him in a few passing words. We put forward the idea, therefore, that Arthur was the 'pole' and 'Master' of a spiritually-operative order of 'knighthood,' and it was this which attracted both Christian and Heathen from all over Northwest Europe to his court**.

The Order of the Round Table may have had an equivalent in Brittany, with close Arthurian ties. Hoel the First of Brittany, also known as Hoel the Great (448-484), was married to Anne, or Enime, daughter of Uther Pendragon, and sister of King Arthur. Hoel is said to have instituted an order of knighthood in Brittany which he called the *Ordre de l'Hermine.*

---

*Compare this with the old Roman Emperors, and the Pope, who have the title of 'pontifex,' or 'bridge-maker' between Heaven and Earth.
**Words cannot describe spiritual greatness except by analogy. This may explain some of the exaggerated claims of Arthur's political and military might, as seen, for example, in Geoffrey of Monmouth's 'History.'

Although the Mabinogion, from Wales, contains some references to Arthur and his court, most of the legends which make up the Arthurian cycle as we know it, come from Brittany. The Bretons must have had a vast wealth of tales and legends about Arthur and his knights, which they had brought over with them as emigrants from the island of Britain in Arthurian, and post-Arthurian times. One only has to look at the three volumes of legends, many of them clearly pre-Christian in origin, collected from the Breton oral tradition by Luzel as late as the nineteenth century, to accept this as a real possibility. It would seem, however, that by the twelfth century when the Arthurian tales came at last to be written down, some legends of the old Celtic deity Artaius may have become confused with the historical Arthur, some ancient heroes not originally linked with Arthur may have been woven into the cycle, and the tales as a whole had been embellished with descriptive passages based on the model of the court of Charlemagne, and also on twelfth century styles. These changes should not necessarily be regretted, for it is the image of the mediaeval knight in panoply, and all the rest, which has given the stories their romantic appeal and permitted them to survive right down to our times. Embellishing stories in this way is not fundamentally harmful, provided the basic symbolism is retained unchanged. Furthermore, the embellishment has helped to make the stories attractive and understandable to a new audience.

At least one historian, Markale, is of the opinion that Lancelot was a non-Arthurian hero, probably a Gaul and not a Briton, who was interpolated into the cycle. Walter Map and Chretien de Troyes were the first to introduce Lancelot into the cycle, but we cannot know if their oral sources already showed him in an Arthurian setting, or not. One thing that is striking, is that the Lancelot episodes in the Grail Legend, and elsewhere in the Arthurian Saga, stand generally as separate stories, independent of much of the rest. Fiction, of course, is often truth-bearing, and the Lancelot of the Grail Legend rings 'true.' There is also something puzzling about Lancelot, the knight of knights betraying the king by having a love affair with his wife, especially considering the strong sense of loyalty and chastity seen in other legends such as Sir Gawain and the Green Knight. On the other hand, there is the story of Tristan and Isoude which sets a kind of precedent for an affair between a knight and his queen, but it was justified in their case because of the magic love-potion. One is left wondering whether the Lancelot-Guenevere part of the Arthurian Saga came down from ancient oral tradition, or was invented by the twelfth century romantic writers. It is possible that the latter needed to have a moral cause for the downfall of Arthur's dynasty, not necessarily for themselves, but to make it understandable to their readers. An older view of this downfall, hinted at in the Grail Legend itself, is that it was time for this particular phase of Celtic history to draw to a close, the Arthurian epoch being like a last rose of summer.

One does not, of course, have to decide on these points; the best conclusion is perhaps to keep an open mind. Whether the Lancelot of the Arthurian Saga is fact or fiction is of little real importance; what matters is that in the Saga he represents the ideal of knighthood, the flower of chivalry.

'There is nothing new under the sun.' The idea of the Quest of the Grail is much older than the Arthurian legend. There are, for example, many older legends from Ireland of the quest of a stone, or a cauldron of abundance. This does not relegate the Arthurian Quest to pure fiction, for the true quest which is symbolised in the tales is re-enacted with each spiritually-orientated generation.

Symbolically, the grail - the vessel which, in the Christian legend, contained the blood of Christ - represents the human 'heart' in the spiritual sense, seen as a spiritual receptacle. Seeing the outside of the grail corresponds therefore with reaching the Primordial State of True Man, accomplishing the lesser mysteries of classical antiquity. Seeing the inside of the grail represents the greater mysteries, experiencing the superior states represented by the Heavens, and on towards Divine Union. Of this ultimate state, the old Chinese Sages said, "words cannot describe it," and that is why the grail, especially the pre-Christian grail is represented like a talisman having wonderful and magical properties, for there is no other way of describing the superior spiritual states than by analogies which suit the mentality of the listener or reader.

The grail is accompanied by a lance; a lance which drips blood, said in the Christian Legend to be the lance which pierced Christ's side. This lance signifies the 'pole,' or spiritual axis. We have already mentioned the symbolism of heart and spiritual axis in connection with boat-building, and the microcosmic symbolism of the army heirarchy. In Christian terms, the blood represents Christ's sacrifice. In general terms, it represents the sacrifice of the spiritual way, for in a sense the death of the ego is a sacrifice of something dear - one's own dear self - even if at a later stage this 'self' is realized to be an illusion.

We have mentioned that the Arthurian Quest of the Grail originates from Brittany. One outstanding piece of evidence that the story was not simply invented by certain twelfth century writers comes from the tale of Peredur, in the Mabinogion, a tale of Welsh origin which has come down to us quite separately from those of Breton origin. Peredur was a seventh son, seven being considered a number of destiny. His six elder brothers had all been killed in combat, and his mother, fearing a similar fate for him, brought him up as a rustic in the forest, with no knowledge of weapons or knighthood. One day, he saw three knights from Arthur's court, and became filled with the desire to imitate them. Seeing no alternative, his mother gave him her blessing and sent him off to Arthur's court. He set out armed only with a few pointed stakes and, on his arrival, slew a knight who had challenged the whole court. Then he set out again like a knight seeking adventure. One day, he came to a castle beside a lake, where there was a venerable old man with attendants who were busy fishing. The old man got up and went into the castle; Peredur followed him, noting he was lame. The old man greeted him hospitably, and promised to teach him how to fight with the sword, and all knightly accomplishments, adding that he was his uncle on his mother's side. He advised Peredur to ride out again, and, should he see anything which caused him wonder, not to ask the meaning of it, thereby giving Peredur a test of obedience and self-restraint. Next, Peredur came to a vast deserted forest, and at the other side he found a great Castle of Wonders. He went through the open door and was honourably received by a stately old man. At dinner, the lord of the castle asked Peredur if he could use a sword, to which he replied that he thought he could if only he were to receive instruction. The lord gave Peredur a sword, telling him to strike at a great iron staple in the floor. After three blows, the old man told Peredur that he had reached two-thirds of his strength, adding that he also was his uncle, and brother to the Fisher-Lord where Peredur had spent the previous day. Whilst they were talking, two youths carried a mighty spear or lance through the hall, its point dripping blood. Next, two maidens came by with a silver dish on which was a bloody head, and there was wailing and moaning. Peredur remembered the injunction of the Fisher-Lord, and asked no questions. Then he set forth again, and had many adventures. At the end of the tale he learnt that the head on the dish was his cousin's. The latter had been slain by the lance he had seen, the result of evil work by the nine sorceresses of Gloucester. With Arthur's help, Peredur attacked the sorceresses and killed them all.

The first part of the tale of Peredur contains many elements found in the Quest of the Grail; Peredur can be identified with Perceval; the Fisher-Lord with the Fisher-King of the Grail Legend; the Castle of Wonders with the Grail Castle; and the lance dripping blood is common to both legends. The Castle of Wonders is situated on the other side of a vast deserted forest, no doubt implying the boundary between this world, and the 'other world' of the psyche. The castle is therefore not necessarily to be identified with any in this world. All that is missing from the tale of Peredur, is the grail itself; in Peredur it seems to have been replaced by the macabre severed head, making the story one of rightful vengeance and redemption. The tale of Peredur may represent the quest of a pre-Christian grail; it may have been modified, perhaps from a Christian desire to remove a pagan element, turning it thereby into a simple tale of revenge and suppression of evil. It is possible that a version of the tale of Peredur may have influenced the origin of some of the Breton tales of the Quest of the Grail. It is likely, however, that the tale of Peredur, in its present form, has come down to us separately, from an older, common source.

A pre-Christian origin of the grail does not mean that the Quest of the Grail is not a Christian legend. The symbolism of the heart as spiritual centre, linked with the spiritual axis, pole, or solar ray, is world-wide; its exteriorisation as a stone or a vessel associated with a lance is therefore applicable to more than one period. The spiritual journey, which can be symbolised first as a journey

18. Illustrations to Peredur
(after Lady Guest's Mabinogion, 1877).

to the outside of the heart, exteriorised as the outside of the Grail, and then on towards the centre, has been accomplished in one generation after another, wherever and whenever man has been spiritually-orientated. The story is therefore just as truly Christian, as pre-Christian. We shall see that this is implied in the Quest of the Grail itself.

The Legend states that for a long time the Holy Grail was visible to all pilgrims, and that its presence conferred blessings on the land where it was kept. Eventually, one of the holy men who guarded it, forgot his sacred office, and looked with lustful eyes on a young female pilgrim. The sacred lance punished him of its own accord, inflicting a deep wound between the thighs; one which would not heal and which rendered him impotent. He therefore became known as *Le Roi Pecheur*, which has the double meaning of Sinner-King and Fisher-King. This part of the story may go back to ancient times when the fertility of the land was considered to depend on the king's virility. After this event, the Holy Grail withdrew its presence from the crowds, and an Iron Age succeeded to the period of happiness which its presence had diffused amongst the tribes of Britain.

This part of the legend can be interpreted in two ways, which are not mutually contradictory. The wider interpretation is that the spiritual way was easily accessible to all in an ancient, far-off Golden Age, but that in this later Age of Iron, it is hidden and difficult of access. The narrower interpretation is Christian, and historical, implying that the earliest Christians had easy access to the spiritual way, but that later, when Christianity had become an exoteric and 'official' religion, the way represented by the Grail was accessible only to those with the requisite esoteric aptitude.

The Quest of the Grail

The story begins with a message announcing the start of the quest, sent by Merlin to King Arthur. Merlin was by then invisible to mortal eyes, but he could still speak to those who approached his invisible prison. He sent the message by Sir Gawain, adding that a knight was already born and of a suitable age to accomplish the quest.

The story continues: One day, at Pentecost, when King Arthur and his knights were seated at the round table,

19. The quest
(by David Lewis).

there was a clap of thunder, and every knight seemed to look fairer than ever before. The hall was filled with perfume, and each had the meat and drink he liked best. Then the Holy Grail, covered in fine white silken cloth so that none could see it directly, passed through the hall and disappeared. During this time no one spoke a word, but when they had recovered, King Arthur said they should thank God for what they had seen. Then Sir Gawain rose up and vowed that he would seek the grail for a year and a day. On hearing this, most of the other knights of the Round Table vowed likewise. "Alas!" said King Arthur to Sir Gawain, "with the vow and promise you have made, you have deprived me of the fairest fellowship that ever were seen together, for I am sure that those who depart shall never all meet again in this world."

At that time an old man came into the hall, and with him he brought a young knight; he greeted the assembly, and then he said to King Arthur: "Sir, I bring you here a young knight that is of king's lineage, and of the kindred of Joseph of Arimathea, being the son of Dame Elaine, the daughter of King Pelles." Now the name of the young knight was Sir Galahad*, and he was the son of Sir Lancelot; but he had been raised by his mother, at the court of King Pelles. Now that he was old enough to bear arms, his mother had sent him in the charge of a holy hermit to King Arthur's court. Then Sir Lancelot beheld his son, which gave him great pleasure. And Sir Bohort predicted that he should come to something great. The queen heard about the new knight, and she went to see him. She and her ladies said that he much resembled his father, and that his features were such as one might not find in the whole world. And King Arthur said: "God make him a good man, for he has as much beauty as anyone alive."

Then the hermit led the young knight to the Seat of Danger; and he lifted up the cloth and found there letters that said: "This is the seat of Sir Galahad, the good knight;" and he made him sit in the seat. And all the

---

*Our version of the Quest is based on 'La Queste del Saint Graal' from the Vulgate Cycle, via Malory. This version is permeated by Cistercian ideals and it introduces a new character, Sir Galahad, as the foremost hero. There is every reason to believe, however, that in the earlier, but incomplete versions of the Quest, Perceval, and possibly also Gawain were envisaged as the foremost heroes.

knights of the Round Table marvelled greatly when they
saw him sit securely in the seat. They said he must be
the one destined to achieve the quest, for none had ever
sat there before without being harmed.

On the next day, the king said that they should hold a
last tournament in the meadow at Camelot, before they
should depart, for they would never all assemble together
again. This gave the king an opportunity to see Galahad
in action. The latter armed himself, but refused to take
any shield, and yet he broke many spears and won over
all the knights he encountered, except Lancelot and Perceval. Then the king made him dismount, and presented
him to the queen, commenting that he resembled his
father so much that it was no wonder he was like him in
prowess.

Then they all went to the minster, and after the mass
the knights put on their helms and departed, and there
was great sorrow. They rode through the streets of Camelot, and there was weeping of the rich and poor. And so
they departed, and every knight took the way he thought
best.

Sir Galahad rode forth without a shield, and he went
four days without finding an adventure. And on the fourth
day he came to a white abbey; and there he was received
with great reverence and led to a chamber. There he met
two knights, King Bagdemagus and Sir Uwaine. Galahad
asked them what adventure had brought them there, and
they told him that there was a shield there which no man
could bear unless he was worthy of it. They added that
if anyone were to bear it who was unworthy, it would
surely do him a mischief. King Bagdemagus said he was
not afraid to try it, and that they would see him do so in
the morning.

So next morning they arose and heard mass; then King
Bagdemagus asked where the adventurous shield was. A
monk led him behind an altar where the shield hung; a
shield as white as snow, with a red cross in the middle.
King Bagdemagus took the shield and went outside, asking
Galahad if he would wait there to see how he fared.

Then King Bagdemagus and his squire rode forth; and
when they had ridden a mile or two, they saw a goodly
knight approaching, in white armour, horse and all; and
he came as fast as his horse could run, with his spear in
the rest; and King Bagdemagus directed his spear against

him, breaking it on the white knight, but the other struck him so hard that he penetrated his right shoulder, for the shield did not protect him. He fell from his horse, and the white knight turned and rode away.

Then the squire went to King Bagdemagus and asked him whether he were wounded or not, to which he replied that he was sore wounded and would be lucky to escape death. Then the squire set him on his horse and took him to an abbey, where they looked after him for a long time, for he had only just escaped with his life. And the squire took the shield back to the abbey.

The next day Galahad took the shield, and within a while he came to a hermitage, where he met the white knight, and each saluted the other courteously. Galahad asked the other to tell him the marvel of the shield. The other replied that it had belonged to Joseph of Arimathea, who had predicted before he died that no man should wear it without regret, until Sir Galahad, the last of his lineage, should come and perform many marvellous deeds. Then the white knight disappeared.

Meanwhile, Sir Gawain had been riding for many a long day, until at last he came to the abbey where Galahad took the white shield. They told him about this, and he said he was sorry he had not accompanied Galahad. But one of the monks warned him that he was too sinful to be in the company of such a man. The monk said that he should do penance for his sins, but Gawain declined, saying that adventurous knights such as he, suffered woe and pain enough as it was. And so he went on his way.

Not long after this, Gawain was riding in the company of Hector, and they came to a castle where there was a great tournament. And Gawain and Hector joined with the party which seemed weaker, and they drove the other party before them. Then suddenly there came into the lists a white knight, bearing a white shield with a red cross, and by chance he came by Gawain, and he struck him so hard that he broke his helm, and wounded him in the head. And Gawain fell to the ground. When Hector saw this, he knew that the knight with the white shield was Sir Galahad, and he thought it unwise to joust with him, the more so because he was his uncle. So Galahad retired, and no one knew where he had gone. And Hector raised up Gawain, and said: "Sir, it seems to me that your quest is done." "It is done," said Gawain; "I shall seek no further*." Then they carried Gawain into the castle, and they found a physician to care for his wound. And Hector and Gawain stayed together, for Hector would not leave until Gawain had recovered.

Now we come to Sir Lancelot, whose quest took him to a wide forest, where he ignored the paths and rode as wild adventure led him. He came at last to a stone cross, and he looked around him and saw an old chapel. He tied his horse to a tree; and then he went up to the chapel and looked through a place where the wall was broken. And inside he saw a fair altar, richly arrayed with silk; and there was a silver candlestick bearing six great candles. When Lancelot saw this sight, he had a great wish to enter the chapel, but he could find no way in. Then he felt heavy and full of dismay; and he went back to his horse, took off his saddle and bridle, and let him graze; and he unlaced his helm, took off his sword, and laid himself down to sleep on his shield, before the cross.

And as he lay, half waking and half sleeping, he saw two fair and white palfreys pass by, bearing a litter on which lay a sick knight. And when he was near the cross, Lancelot heard him say: "Sweet Lord, when shall this sorrow leave me, and when shall the holy vessel come by me whereby I shall be healed?" And thus the knight complained a great while, and Lancelot heard it. Then Lancelot saw the great candlestick, with lighted candles, come before the cross, but he could see no one carrying it. And there came a salver of silver and the Holy Grail; and the sick knight sat upright, and raised his hands, saying: "Fair sweet Lord, which is here within the holy vessel, hear me that I may be cured of this great malady." And he went on hands and knees towards it, and touched and kissed it. And he was cured. Then the holy vessel went into the chapel again, with the candlestick, so that Lancelot knew not what became of it.

*In this version of the Quest, which dates from the early thirteenth century, Gawain is shown as a failure; and some of the later French romances depict him in a bad light. This stands in sharp contrast to Chretien de Troye's unfinished twelfth century version, in which Gawain is described as lord of the knights. We shall see in the next chapter that the author of Sir Gawain and the Green Knight also shows him as an exemplary type. It is possible that Gawain's character was changed by later writers who wished to supplant him in favour of new heroes.

Then the sick knight kissed the cross, and his squire brought him his arms, and asked him how he was. "I thank God right heartily," he said, "for, through the holy vessel, I have been healed. But I have great marvel of this sleeping knight, who had neither grace nor power to awake whilst the holy vessel was here." "I dare say," said the squire, "that this same knight must be stained with some deadly sin." And so they departed.

Then Lancelot awoke, sat upright, and thought of what he had seen, whether it had been a dream, or not. And he felt heavy and did not know what to do. And he said: "My sin and wretchedness has brought me into great dishonour. For when I sought worldly adventures and worldly desires, I always achieved them, and always did well, and was never beaten in a quarrel, whether I was in the right or the wrong. And now that I take on a holy adventure, I can see that my old sin holds me back." And he lamented so till it was day and he heard the dawn chorus. Then he was somewhat comforted.

Then he left the cross and went into the forest. And there he found a hermitage, and he asked the hermit to hear his confession. The latter agreed willingly; and then he told him about his life, and how he had loved a queen unmeasurably for many years. "And all my great deeds of arms that I have done, I did the most part for the queen's sake, and for her sake would I do battle, were it right or wrong, and never did I fight only for God's sake, but to win praise; and little or nought I thanked God for it. I beg you to counsel me." "I will counsel you," said the hermit, "if you will promise me that you will avoid the queen's company." And then Lancelot promised that he would no longer seek her company. "See that your heart and your tongue agree," said the good man, "and I can guarantee that you will have more praise than ever you had before." And he gave him a penance to do.

Now we turn to Sir Perceval's quest. He set out and rode till noon; and he met in a valley about twenty men at arms. And when they saw Perceval they asked him where he came from; and he answered: "From the court of King Arthur." Then they all cried: "Kill him." But Sir Perceval struck the first one to the ground, and his horse on top of him. Then seven of them struck on his shield all at once, and the others his horse, so that he fell to the ground. He would have been killed had not the good

113

knight Galahad, with his red cross, come there by chance. And when he saw all the knights attacking one, he cried out: "Save me that knight's life." Then he rode towards the men at arms as fast as he could, with his spear in the rest, and he struck down the foremost knight, and his horse. And when his spear was broken, he drew his sword and struck out marvellously to right and to left, putting them to flight, and pursuing them into the forest. And when Perceval saw him chasing them, he lamented that his horse was slain, and he cried out to the knight, whom he thought was Galahad; but the latter had gone so fast that he soon passed out of sight. Perceval gave himself up to his sadness, staying there all day, and sleeping there until, at midnight, he awoke to see a beautiful woman. She asked him what he was doing there, to which he replied that he was doing "neither good, nor great ill." And then she offered to lend him her horse, on condition that he would do what she asked if she summoned him. He agreed, and she went to fetch him her horse. And she returned with a beast which was inky black; a great horse and well-apparelled. Perceval marvelled at it, and leapt upon its back with no further thought. He dug his spurs in, and in an hour it had taken him four days' journey from there. He came to rough water, which roared; and the horse would have taken him into it, but on seeing the danger, Perceval made the sign of the cross on his forehead. This caused the fiendly beast to shake him off, just before it went into the water crying and roaring. Then Perceval realized it was a fiend that would have caused his downfall, and he commended himself to God; and he stayed there praying all night. In the morning he saw that he was in a wild place, and surrounded by the sea. And he looked out to sea, and saw a ship coming towards him; and it came and stood still under a rock. And when Perceval saw this, he went there and found the ship was covered in silk, and within it there was a lady of great beauty, clothed in the richest garments.

And when she saw Perceval, she greeted him. He, in his turn, asked her of her country and of her lineage. She replied that she had once been the richest woman in the world, but that she had been disinherited. "Damsel," said Percival, "who has disinherited you? for I pity you very much." "Sir," she said, "my enemy is a great and powerful lord, and he used to make a great fuss of me, so that

I came to have a little more pride than I ought to have had; also, I said something which displeased him; so he drove me from his company, and from my heritage. Therefore, if you are the good knight you seem to be, I beg you to help me."

Then Perceval promised her all the help that he could, and she thanked him.

The weather was hot, and she called her maid and had her pitch a pavilion on the gravel. "Sir," she said, "now you may rest in the heat of the day." Then he thanked her, and she took off his helm, and he slept there a great while. Then he awoke and asked her if she had any meat, and she said yes; and she had all kinds of meats set out on the table. And he drank there the strongest wine he had ever tasted, and when he beheld the lady he thought she was the fairest creature he ever had seen. And he offered her love and begged her to be his. She refused him in such a way that made his desire more ardent. And when he kept on insisting, she said she would not give him her love unless he promised to be her servant and do only as she commanded. He agreed, but as he spoke he saw his sword lying on the floor, with the sign of the cross on the pommel. Then he made the sign of the cross on his forehead and the pavilion withered and changed into smoke, forming a black cloud. And the damsel cried aloud and ran to her ship; it sailed away with the wind roaring, and the water seemed to be burning in its wake. Then Perceval was sorrowful on realizing he had almost lost, and he took his arms and departed from there.

Now we turn to Sir Bohort, or Bors for short. When he set out from Camelot he met with a religious man riding on an ass; and Bors saluted him. "Who are you?" said the good man. "Sir," said Bors, "I am a knight who would be counselled in the quest of the Holy Grail." So they rode together till they came to a hermitage; and there Bors alighted and spent the night with him. He was confessed, and then they ate bread and drank water together. The good man advised him to eat no other kind of food until he should sit at the table of the Holy Grail. Bors asked him how he knew he would be there, and he replied that he knew it well, but that there would not be many of his fellows with him. Bors agreed about the food, and the good man who had heard his confession found him in so pure and stable a life that he marvelled at it.

115

Next day, Bors departed and rode through the forest until midday. And then he met, at the parting of two ways, two knights that led Lionel, his brother, all naked and bound upon a strong horse; and his hands were tied in front of his chest and they were beating him with thorns so that he was all bloody. Bors prepared to rescue his brother, but he looked on the other side and saw a knight dragging a fair maiden who cried out: "Saint Mary! help your maid!" And when she saw Bors, she called to him and said: "By the faith you owe to your knighthood, help me!" When Bors heard her say this, he was upset, for he knew not what to do. "For if I let my brother be, he will be killed, but if I do not help the maid, I shall be shamed forever." Then he lifted his eyes and said: "Lord keep Sir Lionel, my brother, so none of these knights slay him, and for our Lady's sake I will help the maid."

Then he cried out to the knight: "Sir Knight, hands off that maid, or I will kill you." Then the knight set down the maid, took his shield, and drew his sword. And Bors struck him such a blow that it went through his shield and into his left shoulder, and he fell down on the ground. Then Bors went to the maid and told her she was safe. She begged him to take her back to where she had come from, and he did so, leading her on the wounded knight's horse. And there he found twelve knights seeking after her; and when she told them how Bors had rescued her, they were full of joy and asked him to go to her father, a great lord, who would make him welcome. Bors excused himself, saying that he had a great adventure ahead, and so he departed.

Then he rode after Lionel, his brother, following the tracks of their horses. He overtook a man in religious clothing who said: "Sir Knight, what are you seeking?" "Sir," said Bors, "I seek my brother who has been taken by two knights." "Ah, Bors, trouble not to seek for him, for truly he is dead." Then he showed him a freshly-killed body lying in a thick bush; and it seemed to him that it was his brother's body. And then he fell to the ground in a swoon, and lay there for a long time. When he came to, he asked the man the way to some chapel. And the man showed him the way to a chapel, and they both alighted there and put the body in a marble tomb.

Then Bors commended the good man to God, and went on his way. And he rode all that day, and rested the night at an old lady's house. Next morning, he rode to a castle in a valley, and there he met a yeoman. "Tell me," said Bors, "do you know of any adventure?" "Sir," he said, "a great tournament is going to be held beneath these castle walls." Then Bors thought to be there, for some of the fellowship of the quest of the grail might also be there. So he turned towards a hermitage that was on the edge of the forest, and when he got there, he found Lionel his brother, in full armour outside the chapel door. When he saw his brother, Bors greeted him with great joy; but his brother's reply was to threaten him with death for having helped the maiden instead of himself. Bors went down on his knees before his brother, but the latter insisted that they must fight. Bors thought it best not to do so, but his brother rode at him as he knelt on the ground, and his horse's hoofs knocked him flat. Then Lionel dismounted so that he might strike off his brother's head; but before he could do so, Sir Colgrevance, a knight of the Round Table, came on the scene, took hold of Lionel by the shoulders, and drew him back from his brother. He said to him: "Lionel, will you slay your brother?" "Why," said Lionel, "will you prevent me? If you interfere, I will slay you first, and then him." And he ran to strike Bors, but Colgrevance put himself between them, saying: "If you persist any more, we two shall fight one another." Then Lionel defied him and gave him a great stroke through the helm. Then he drew his sword and defended himself manfully. Whilst the fight was going on, Bors began thinking that if his brother were slain he should have no joy, and if his brother slew Colgrevance, he would be shamed forever.

Then he tried to rise to part them, but he did not have the strength to do it. Then Colgrevance cried out to Bors for help, but as he did so, Lionel struck off his helm and killed him. Then he rushed fiendishly at his brother and gave him a stroke which made him stoop. And Bors said: "For God's sake, leave this battle, for if it happened, fair brother, that I killed you, or you me, we sould be dead of that sin." "Don't ask me for mercy," said Lionel. Then Bors drew his sword, saying "God have mercy on me;" but just as he lifted it high, he heard a voice which said: "Flee, Bors, and don't touch him." And at the same time a fiery cloud came between them, which caused them to faint on the ground. When they came to, Bors saw that his brother was unharmed, for he feared that God might have taken vengeance on him. Then Lionel said: "Brother, forgive me all that I have done to you, for God's sake." And Bors said: "God forgive you, as I do."

Then Bors heard a voice that said: "Make your way to the sea, for Perceval awaits you there." So he departed and rode straight towards the sea. He came to an abbey that was near the sea, and he thought to rest the night there; but whilst he was sleeping, a voice told him to go to the seashore. He got up, made the sign of the cross on his forehead, and armed himself. Then he took his horse and rode out through a break in the wall, and came to the seashore. And there he found a ship, all covered in white silken cloth. And he went on board, but it was so dark that he could see no one, and he laid himself down and slept till daybreak. Then he woke up and saw, in the middle of the ship, a knight all armed, except for his helm; and he recognized him as Perceval, and the sight of each other gave them great joy. Then Perceval said: "All we lack now is Sir Galahad."

Now the story returns to Sir Lancelot. It happened that one night Lancelot arrived before a castle, which was rich and fair. And there was a rear entrance which was open and guarded only by two lions. And it was a clear moonlit night. Whilst he was there, he heard a voice that said: "Lancelot, go into the castle, where you shall see a great part of what you desire." So he went to the gate, but he drew his sword when he saw the two lions. Then something invisible struck his arm so hard that his sword fell from his hands, and he heard a voice say: "O man of evil faith, why do you believe more in your arms than in your Maker?" Then Lancelot thanked God for his mercy in reproving his misdeed, and for such a sign that showed him to be God's servant. Then he made a cross on his forehead and went to the lions; and they menaced him, but they let him pass unharmed and he went into the castle. Inside, he found that all the gates and doors were open, until finally, he came to a door that was shut, and he tried to open it, but he could not. Then he listened and heard a voice which sung so sweetly that it seemed no earthly thing; and a voice said: "Joy and honour be to the Father of Heaven," Then Lancelot kneeled down before the chamber, for he well knew that the Holy Grail was inside. Then he prayed to God to permit him to see something of what he was seeking. And with that he saw the door open; and a bright light shone from it so that it seemed as though all the torches in the world were there. He went to the door, and would have gone in, but a voice said to him: "Stay, Lancelot, and do not enter." And he drew back, and felt heavy in his mind. Then he looked into the room, and saw a silver table, and the holy vessel covered with red silk, and many angels about it; one of the angels held a lighted candle, and another a cross and the ornaments of the altar. Then, through sheer wonder, Lancelot forgot himself and stepped forward into the room; and suddenly a hot breath struck him so sorely in the face that he fell to the ground and had no strength to rise. Then he felt many hands about him, which lifted him and carried him out of the room, and left him still in a faint outside. When day broke, and the people of the castle were about, they found Lancelot lying before the closed door. And they felt his pulse to see if there were any life left in him. And they found life in him, although he could not move a limb. So they took him to a room and laid him on a bed, where he remained many days. And some of them thought he was dead, but one old man said: "He is as full of life as the mightiest of you, and therefore I advise you to look after him until God brings him back again." And after twenty-four days he opened his eyes; and when he saw the people, he was sorrowful and said: "Why did you wake me? for I was better then than I am now." "What did you see?" they asked him. "I saw great marvels that no tongue can tell, and more than any heart can think." Then they said: "Sir, the quest of the Holy Grail is achieved right now in you, and you shall never see more of it than you have seen." "I thank God," said Lancelot, "of his great mercy, for what I have seen, for it is sufficient for me." Then he got up and dressed; and when they saw him thus, the knew it was Sir Lancelot the good knight. And, after four days, he took his leave of the lord of the castle, and of all the fellowship that were there, and thanked them for having taken care of him. Then he departed and returned to Camelot, where he found King Arthur and Queen Guenevere; but many of the knights of the Round Table had lost their lives. Then he told the king all his adventures on the quest.

Now the story turns to Sir Galahad. When he had rescued Perceval from the twenty knights, he rode into a vast forest, where he spent many days. Then he went towards the sea, and on his way he stayed the night at a hermitage. And the good man was glad when he saw he was a knight-errant. And when they were resting, there came a gentlewoman knocking on the door; and the good man answered the knocking and asked her what she wanted. Then she said: "I would speak with the knight." Then Galahad went to her and asked her what she wanted. "Sir Galahad," she said, "I want you to arm and mount upon your horse, and follow me; for I will show you the highest adventure that any knight ever saw." Then Galahad armed himself, and commended himself to God, and told her to go on in front, and that he would follow wherever she led.

So she rode as fast as her palfrey could go, until she reached the sea; and there they found the ship where Bors and Perceval were waiting. They cried from the ship: "Sir Galahad, you are welcome; we have been expecting you." And when he heard them, he asked the good woman who they were. "Sir," she said, "leave your horse here, and I shall leave mine, and we will join their company." And so they went on board the ship and the two knights received them both with great joy. They knew the good woman, for she was Perceval's sister. Then the wind came up and drove them through the sea all that day, and the next, till the ship came between two great rocks; but they could not land there, for there was a whirlpool; but there was another ship which they could board without danger. "We should go there," said the gentlewoman, "and there we shall see adventures, for such is our Lord's will." Then Galahad went on board, next the gentlewoman, and then Bors and Perceval. And when they were on board, they found the silver table there, with the Holy Grail, which was covered in red silk. And they made great reverence to it, and Galahad prayed a long time, asking that whatever time he should ask to leave this world, he should do so; and a voice told him that his request would be granted, and that when he asked for the death of his body, he would have it, and then he would find the life of the soul.

And shortly the wind came up and drove them across the sea, till they came to the city of Sarras. Then they took the silver table out of the ship, Perceval and Bors at the front, and Galahad behind, and thus they went to the city. And at the gate of the city they saw an old man, a cripple. Then Galahad called him and asked him to help carry this heavy thing. "Truly," said the old man, "It is ten years since I walked without crutches." "Do not worry," said Galahad; "just get up and show your good will." Then the old man got up, and found himself whole; and he ran to the table and took one part with Galahad.

When they went into the city, it happened that the king had just died; and the people were all dismayed and did not know whom to have as their new king. Whilst they were in council, they heard a voice telling them to choose the youngest of the three newly-arrived knights, to be their king. So they made Galahad king, by the full assent of the city. And when he was made king he commanded them to make a chest of gold and precious stones to hold the holy vessel. And every day the three companions went and prayed before it.

Now exactly a year after Galahad had been crowned king, he got up early, and, with his fellows, went before the holy vessel; and they saw one kneeling there who had a great fellowship of angels about him; and he called Sir Galahad and said: "Come, servant of the Lord, and see that which you have so much desired to see." And then Galahad's mortal flesh trembled as he began to see spiritual things. Then the good man said: "Do you know who I am?" "No," said Galahad. "I am Joseph of Arimathea, and God has sent me here to keep you company." Then Galahad held up his hands towards heaven and said: "Now I would no longer live, if it might please God." And when he had said these words, he went to Perceval and Bors, and kissed them, and commended them to God. And then he knelt before the table and prayed, and suddenly his soul departed, and a great multitude of angels carried it up towards heaven, and Perceval and Bors saw it. Then a hand came from heaven and took the holy vessel, and carried it up to heaven, and since that time no one has been so bold as to say he has seen the Holy Grail on earth any more.

(Note: At the end, Galahad has been invited to look into the Holy Grail, which represents the accomplishment of the greater mysteries. For a longer version see P. M. Matarasso's translation in the Penguin Classics series; in that version, it is not Joseph of Arimathea, but his son who invites Galahad to look into the Grail.)

CHAPTER 9. SIR GAWAIN AND THE GREEN KNIGHT.

The Green Knight, or Green Man, is known in legend throughout the world. Although most British writers seem to have ignored him, the occurrence of Green Man inns is witness to his recognition in British folk-lore. At least one European writer, Cervantes, seems to have known him, for he included a meeting with a 'gentleman in green' in Don Quixote. We shall comment on this in the final chapter. The Green Man is often described as the 'King of the World;' sometimes as the 'Eternal Prophet.' It is said that he celebrates his sacred rites underground, and that when he does so, the whole of nature above, stands still and silent. In Islam he is known as Al Khidr. Green is the colour of nature, and it is the colour that symbolises eternity.

There are many traditions concerning him in Islam. He seems to have been the one who advised the companions of the Prophet to use the human voice as a call to prayer, when they were wondering if they should use a bell, like the Christians. Ibn 'Arabi describes meeting him on more than one occasion*. At one of those meetings, Al Khidr came striding across the sea to him; on another occasion he prayed with his body in the air, a few feet above the ground, a miracle aimed at strengthening the faith of one of Ibn 'Arabi's companions. In another story Ibn 'Arabi tells of Al Khidr investing (initiating) a Sufi with a small cloth cap; Austin points out that such initiation by Al Khidr himself is considered to be of the highest kind.

There is a tradition in Islam that whoever wishes to receive a visit from Al Khidr should clean the threshold of his, or her house, and keep it clean for forty days and nights. According to one story, a woman did this, and on the fortieth day an old tramp came along and asked to be let in for a drink of water. She refused him on the pretext that she was expecting an important visitor.When next she looked up, she saw him disappearing over the horizon on a magic carpet! The profound meaning of keeping the threshold of one's house clean is, of course, keeping the mind clean and pure; a simple peasant could perhaps achieve this state solely from the literal act.

*See Austin, R. 'Sufis of Andalusia.'

The high spiritual station of Al Khidr is explained in a passage of the Koran. In the Surah (Chapter) of the Cave, there is an account of a meeting between Moses and a mysterious person generally identified as Al Khidr. Moses asked him if he could go with him, to which he replied that he (Moses) would not be able to bear with him, because he had not the knowledge. Moses said he would be patient and not contradict him. He agreed, asking Moses not to ask about anything until he mentioned it himself. They set out, and came to a boat, and he made a hole in it. Moses at once asked him if he had done this to drown the owners of the boat, adding that surely it was a dreadful thing to do. The other reminded him of his promise, and Moses apologised. Next they met a lad whom he slew, and Moses criticised him saying surely it was a horrid thing to do. Once again he reminded him of his promise, and Moses said that if he did it again, he may leave him. And they went on and came to a town where the people refused them food and hospitality; nevertheless he repaired a wall there which was falling into ruin. Once again, Moses spoke, saying he could have asked payment for repairing the wall.

Then he said they must part, but first he explained to Moses the meaning of the things he could not bear with: He had holed the boat because a king was following and requisitioning all the boats; the owners of the boat would not lose theirs because it was damaged. The lad he killed was unworthy of his parents, and God intended him to be changed for one better. The wall belonged to two orphan boys; there was a treasure beneath it, and it was destined for them when they were old enough. He added that he did these things not of his own will, implying that it was at the Divine Command. This passage also explains why stories of the Green Man are difficult to understand, and why he is sometimes depicted in terrible aspect, or quite misunderstood.

One of the functions of the Green Man, or King of the World, appears to be to 'step in,' providing initiation and functioning as a Spiritual Master, wherever and whenever tradition fails to provide for someone who is qualified by the right spiritual aptitude and orientation. He can therefore be seen as playing a role whenever a tradition is falling into decay and no longer providing an initiatic way for certain types of qualified person; he also fulfils a a role in a viable tradition for those who, for one reason or another, are not provided for*.

The story of Sir Gawain and the Green Knight seems to be set in the early days of King Arthur and his court, before the Quest of the Holy Grail. It may be seen as the Green Knight stepping in and providing Gawain with a special initiatic way. It may perhaps also be seen as Gawain's preparation for the Quest of the Grail, for he is believed by some to have been one of its heroes, and only to have been supplanted later by others, for example Galahad and Lancelot, as we have already pointed out.

Part of the 'plot' of Sir Gawain and the Green Knight, involving a challenge to reciprocal head chopping, is not original; one of the best-known earlier versions is a tale from Ireland concerning Cuchulain, who lived during the reign of Conor mac Nessa:

"A lord of Ulster named Briccriu of the Poisoned Tongue once made a feast to which he invited King Conor and all the heroes. During the feast he set the heroes contending among themselves as to who was champion of Ireland. At last it was agreed that the championship must lie among three of them, namely Cuchulain, Conall of the Victories, and Laery the Triumphant. To decide between these three a demon named The Terrible was summoned from the depths of the lake where he dwelt. He proposed a test of courage to the heroes. Any one of them, he said, might cut off his head today provided the would-be champion would likewise lay his own head on the block the following day. Conall and Laery shrank from the test, but Cuchulain accepted, and, after reciting a charm over his sword, he struck the demon's head off. The demon got up and took the bleeding head in one hand, and his axe in the other, and dived into the lake. Next day he came back all in one piece to claim his part of the bargain. Cuchulain resolutely laid his head on the block. The demon told him to stretch out his neck, which he did, and then he swung

*Many modern readers, brought up with a cult of individualism, may be tempted to imagine themselves falling into one of these categories. We add a word of warning that the very thought of this is likely to be a consequence of a strong individualism and constitute a disqualification.

his axe three times over his victim, finally bringing the butt end down with a crash and bidding Cuchulain rise, unhurt, Champion of Ireland."

This tale from Ireland, however, only contains elements from the beginning and ending of the story of Sir Gawain and the Green Knight. The latter, a Mediaeval English poem from around 1375*, contains a great deal more than the former, for it symbolises the spiritual journey. A few of the many published versions of the story are listed in the bibliography. We summarise it as follows:

Sir Gawain and the Green Knight.

The story begins by setting the scene at the court of King Arthur, one Christmas-tide, at a time when Arthur and his knights were quite young. The poem, in fact, describes them as 'berdlez childer' or beardless youths.

The king, his ladies and knights were about to begin their New Year feast. Bishop Bawdewyn was in the seat of honour, at the head of the table, and Sir Gawain, a nephew of the king, was next to Guenevere. Just as they were about to eat the first course, an awesome figure rode into the banqueting hall. He was fully a head taller than anyone in the court, but, despite his stature, he was handsome and well-proportioned. Everything about him was green; his clothes were bright green with gold adornments. His hair, like his horse's, was of a greenish hue, and it fell over his shoulders like a mantle, running round to his beard; and his hair and beard were trimmed around just above the level of the elbows. Even the metal of his stirrups was enamelled green. He was quite unarmed, except that he carried a huge axe in one hand; in the other he held a holly branch, a sign of peace. His red eyes flashed bright as fire as he looked the assembled knights up and down:

"Where is," he sayd, "the gouenour of this gyng?" meaning where is the governor of this gang, or, in polite modern English, where is the ruler of this assembly? None of the knights dare reply; then Arthur bade him welcome, and invited him to stay. The Green Knight replied that

*The poem is believed, however, to have been based on fragments of oral tradition which were still in circulation at that time.

**20. Wielding the axe,
from the Legend of Cuchulain**
(lino print, David Lewis).

he did not intend to stay, but that he was looking for 'sport,' and he challenged anyone there to give him a blow with his battle-axe, on condition that he might return it after a year and a day.

Seeing that his knights were awestruck, King Arthur himself offered to take up the challenge, but Gawain asked permission to take his place, implying that the business was foolish, and unbecoming for a king.

The king commanded Gawain to rise from the table, and he went and took the axe. King Arthur, for his part, gave Gawain his blessing and advised him to strike resolutely, assuring him that he would survive the other's blow later. The Green Knight asked Sir Gawain to promise that he would seek him out in a year and a day, adding that he would inform him where he lived after the blow had been struck. Then Sir Gawain struck the Green Knight's head off, with a deft stroke of the battle-axe. The Green Knight bent down, picked up his head, and all bleeding, vaulted onto his horse. With his hand he turned his head towards the high table, and charged Gawain to make his way to the Green Chapel to receive his blow, next New Year's morning. He added that many men knew him as the Knight of the Green Chapel, and that if he sought him, he would find him. Then the Green Knight galloped out of the hall, with sparks flying from the stones under his horse's hoofs. Arthur and his knights took up their feasting, and many of them thought it a marvel.

Time went by, and Gawain tarried at Arthur's court. The Michaelmas moon came with its warning of winter, and Gawain began to think about his hazardous quest. Yet he tarried awhile with Arthur, until, on All Saints' Day, he asked leave to go. The next morning they armed him in splendid fashion. The poem describes his shield:

"Then thay schewed hym the shelde...
Wyth the pentangle* depaynt of pure gold hwez...
And quy the pentangle apendez to that prince noble
I am in tent to telle...
...hit is a figure that haldez fyue poyntez.
And vch lyne vmbelappez and loukez in other
And ayquere hit is endlez; and Englych hit callen
Oueral, as I here, the endlez knot."

*See front cover.

(Then they showed him the shield, with the pentangle picked out in pure gold hue... Any why the pentangle belongs to that noble prince, I am intent on telling you... It is a figure which has five points, and each line overlaps and interlocks with another, and nowhere has it an end; and everywhere, as I hear, the English call it the endless knot).

The poet goes on to explain the five points of the pentangle as representing Gawain's five, five-fold virtues; he was faultless in his five senses, there was never a fault through his five fingers, etc.

Gawain spurred his horse, and set out with sparks flying from under its hoofs. He went riding in the name of God through the realm of Logres (England), on to North Wales, and beyond into the wilderness of the Wirral. He asked:

"If thay had herde any karp of a Knyzt Grene,
In any grounde thereabout, of the grene chapel."

But none had heard of the knight, nor the Green Chapel. He went on his way, on unfamiliar paths and in strange regions:

"Sumwhyle wyth wormez he werrez; and wyth wolues
als,
Sumwhile wyth wodwos that woned in the kharrez,
Both with bullez and berez, and borez operquyle,
And etaynez that hym anclede of the heze felle;
Nade he ben duzty and dryze, and Dryztyn had serued,
Douteles he had ben ded and dreped ful ofte."

(Sometimes he fought with dragons, and with wolves also. Sometimes with forest trolls, who lived in the rocks, with bulls and bears too, and at other times with boars, and ogres who pursued him from the fells above*; had he not been bold and unflinching and served God, without doubt he would have been struck down and killed many a time).

On Christmas Eve he prayed to the Virgin Mary for guidance. Suddenly, he saw in the woods, an enchanted castle surrounded by a moat. He spurred Gryngolet, his

*Whitall Perry points out that this part of the poem may be regarded as representing Gawain's descent into Hell.

horse, and reached the end of the drawbridge. He called out to the porter, who went away and soon returned with others. They lowered the drawbridge and Gawain went in and was welcomed by the lord of the castle. He was a man of huge stature, and seemed a bold knight. Gawain introduced himself, and the lord seemed pleased to know who he was, saying:

"He watz the welcomest wyze of the world."

(he was the most welcome man in the world).

The lady of the castle also came to greet him; she seemed fairer even than Guenevere; she was led by another venerable old lady who was not so pleasant to behold. And they spent a festive evening together.

The next three days were spent in the manner of the festive season. Then the lord asked Gawain his reason for travelling at that unusual time of the year. Gawain told him of his tryst, or covenant with the Green Knight, adding that he must now be on his way. The lord assured him that he could stay until the first day of the year, for, he said, the Green Chapel was close at hand. He promised to set him on the right road early on New Year's morning, and assured him he would be there by mid-morning.

Sir Gawain was pleased to hear this news, and he agreed to stay and do whatever the lord of the castle asked of him. The lord told him that as he had travelled long and hard, he should rest in bed in the mornings, and spend each of the next three days in the company of his beautiful wife, until he returned from his daily hunting. The lord proposed a tryst; whatever he took hunting in the woods should be Gawain's, and whatever Gawain obtained in the castle should be his. Gawain agreed.

On the first morning, the lord went out hunting, and Gawain lay in bed. The lady came into his room, and seated herself on his bedside. She spent a long time in conversation, trying to tempt him. This gave Gawain the problem of keeping his knightly vows and not betraying his host's trust, and at the same time resisting the lady's advances without offending her. She even tried taunting him, and finally Gawain ended up accepting a single kiss. The lord returned and offered Gawain the venison he had caught. Gawain was obliged, in return, to kiss the lord on the neck, giving him what he had received that day.

Next day the lady tempted and tested Gawain again. Once more he was in a quandary of not wishing to betray his host, not wishing to offend the lady, and having to make tremendous efforts to control his own passions. Once more, she gave him a kiss, and when the lord returned and offered Gawain the wild boar's meat he had taken, he had to kiss him again, in return.

The same thing happened on the third day, except that, having tempted Gawain sorely, the lady persuaded him to accept a love token, or keepsake. First she offered him a valuable ring, which he refused; then she persuaded him to accept a thing of lesser value, a length of green silk. She told him that it would protect him from harm, and she asked him to keep it secret from her husband. He agreed, and then she kissed him three times. When the lord returned, Gawain gave him the three kisses he had received, but he kept the green silk a secret. The lord implied that he had done better than himself, saying:

> "For I haf hunted all this day, and nozt haf I geten
> Bot this foule fox felle."

And he showed him a miserable fox skin.

On New Year's morning the lord provided Gawain with a guide to put him on the way to the Green Chapel. They set off, over hill and crag, and the guide attempted to put him off his quest, by describing the Green Knight as:

> "...the worst vpon erthe
> For he is stiffe and sterne, and to strike louies,
> And more he is then any mon vpon myddelerde,
> And his body bigger than the best fowre
> That in Arthurez hous..."

The guide failed to dissuade Sir Gawain, and he turned back, leaving him to go on alone to the Green Chapel, which was a green mound, all hollow inside. Gawain called out a challenge. "Wait," replied the Green Knight, "and you shall quickly have all that I once promised you." He soon appeared, all green and wielding a huge Danish axe. He greeted Gawain with the words:

> "...God the mot loke!
> Iwysse thou art welcom, wyze, to my place."

(God keep you! You are truly welcome, sir, to my dwelling*). And he added that now it was his turn to strike. Gawain bowed his head and bared his neck. Just as the Green Knight was bringing down his axe, Gawain flinched, and he stopped short. The second time he stopped short again, but he brought the axe down a third time, just nicking Gawain's neck so that his blood stained the snow.

The Green Knight then explained that the three strokes were for the three days of their tryst during his stay at the castle; he stopped short on the first two strokes because Gawain had told him the truth on the first two days; he had nicked his neck on the third stroke because Gawain had only told him part of the truth on the third day, when he had given him the three kisses but not the green silk. Gawain was ashamed of having kept the silken girdle a secret from him, and thus having broken the tryst. The Green Knight, on the other hand, praised him, saying that he was absolved and purged clean of his offence; clean as if he had never sinned since the day he was born**. And he added that truly he seemed to him the most faultless knight who ever lived. He gave him the green silk girdle to wear, and Gawain agreed to wear it, not for his merits, but to remind him of his shame over breaking the tryst.

The Green Knight implied that the adventure had been instigated by Morgan the Fay, who lived in his dwelling and who was Arthur's half-sister and Gawain's aunt. Once more, the Green Knight complimented him for his honesty and then Gawain set out on the return journey to Arthur's court. When he arrived there, he recounted his adventures with great humility. Because he was wearing the green band diagonally as a sign of shame, others at the court did likewise for his sake.

---

*This is hardly the greeting one would expect of a man just described by Gawain's guide as "the worst vpon erthe," and we must conclude that the guide, who was the Green Knight's servant, was simply trying to put him off. The Green Man is known by many different names; one of them is said to be Melchisedec, who, in the Old Testament, was 'priest of the Most High God;' once again this underlines the high spiritual nature of his function.

**This implies Gawain's return to the primordial state of True Man. It also helps to explain Christ's words: "Except ye be converted, and become as little children, ye shall not enter into the kingdom of heaven." Matthew XVIII, 3.

CHAPTER 10. AFTER THE MIDDLE AGES.

The passage from the Middle Ages to the Renaissance was clear and abrupt, for it represented a total change from an inward-looking attitude, to one of looking outwards at the world. The reason the Middle Ages later came to be seen as the Dark Ages was because the change in attitudes and outlook produced a new type of person, to whom the Middle Ages seemed obscure simply because they could not understand them. This is not meant to imply that the Middle Ages were perfect; they represented a period when the ideals of the spiritual way were subscribed to, but which was far from ideal in other respects. The Middle Ages had to end, if for no other reason than the almost continual warfare and power struggles of the kings and princes of Europe was in flat contradiction to their claim to belong to Christendom.

The change in attitudes following the Middle Ages can be illustrated with reference to poverty, taken in its original sense of having few possessions, rather than one of being destitute and miserable. In the Middle Ages the poor man was esteemed for living up to a Christian ideal, concentrating on things spiritual rather than worldly. Around the end of the Middle Ages, many British aristocrats found there was money to be made by running large flocks of sheep. Their attitude to their poor subsistence tenants changed. The poor man was seen as such because he was a lazy man; this gave the excuse to drive him off the land, obliging him to become a city slum-dweller. By the time the Puritans came along, the poor man was seen by the worst of them as poor because he was being punished by God for his sins, an inversion of the attitude of the Middle Ages.

Although we have said that the passage from the Middle Ages to the Renaissance was clear and abrupt, it is not possible to put a date on it, for the Middle Ages persisted longer in some places, and amongst some groups of people, than others. One significant date, however, was in May 1312 when Philip the Fair of France instigated the destruction of the Templars. The latter order had been founded in 1118 under the guidance of St Bernard. They had the aim of guarding the routes to the Holy Land, which can be taken literally, but also in a more profound sense. Their activities put them in contact with other civilisations. They seem to have formed an intellectual link between East and West, and to have become the guardians of a great deal of esoteric knowledge. Philip the Fair's investigators forced many of the Templars to confess to superstitions and excesses. The Templars as a whole were probably not guilty of the things of which they were accused. It is possible, however, that the order may have been infiltrated by a minority who were misusing it on the lines of the accusations. A purge might have been in order, but Philip's action in destroying the order was like throwing out the baby with the bath water, a baby which was, moreover, central to the intellectual and esoteric corpus of Christianity.

Although some fine monasteries were built during the Renaissance, the esoteric element went into decline. Deprived of a strong intellectual and esoteric corpus, Christianity became entrenched, taking a harder, and more fundamental line. An insistence on a literal interpretation of rites led some, such as Luther, to break away from the established Church, a break which could possibly have been avoided had the latter been able to put forward a more esoteric argument.

The changes we have outlined resulted in more people seeking an esoteric way outside the official body of the Church; they also resulted in a need for organisations having an initiatic character, to become, or remain, strictly secret. The craft initiations had a built-in character of secrecy, for their symbolic language was also the everyday practical language of the craft. They were, however, not open to anyone, but only practitioners of the particular craft; moreover, not all of them went beyond the first part of the spiritual quest, the 'lesser mysteries.' The blacksmiths' initiation, for example, fell into the latter category. One of the craft organisations, masonry, made a sacrifice by opening its door to others who were not practising the craft. In doing this, masonry accepted many genuine seekers who no doubt benefited from it, and who otherwise might not have found a way; the sacrifice it made, however, was that this wider intake carried the risk of eventual infiltration by persons who might weaken or misuse it. Last century, Tolstoy tried freemasonry in Russia, and he came to the conclusion that it was no longer spiritually-operative there. Masonry has, however, kept its symbolism, which is said to be in its most intact form in Scotland. Most of the other craft initiations were weakened or destroyed by the Industrial Revolution. A notable exception, the *Compagnonnage* in France, a guild of constructors in timber, is said to have survived intact until modern times as a very closed organisation.

Apart from the craft societies, there were other secret organisations. We have already mentioned an older one in connection with Dante. Amongst such societies, the Rose Cross is perhaps the best known; there must have been others of which we know nothing at all. Many of the craft, and other secret societies met in inns and taverns, partly because they were often the only meeting places available, and partly because they provided a front to disguise their spiritual nature. The song: 'There's a tavern in the town...' would seem to come from such an initiatic organisation, the reference to 'my true love' being capable of transposition from the barmaid to something more profound, and the words 'I can no longer stay with thee' and the 'weeping willow tree' can be transposed from the literal to one of spiritual death and rebirth, for the willow is a sign of death or mourning. There are, of course, many other old love songs which are capable of a profound interpretation.

Alchemy also flourished after the Middle Ages. Just like the secret societies meeting in taverns, alchemy had its own front and cover in its literal aim of seeking gold, as well as its language. In the earlier chapters of this book we have quoted some examples from alchemical texts of the period, sufficient to give the reader a good idea of what true alchemy was about.

Although many initiatic societies had to function as underground movements during the Renaissance and Post-Renaissance periods, there was, in a sense, a liberation in the philosophical field, for the Renaissance had included a revival of interest in the writings of classical antiquity. We have quoted from some of the English Platonists in the earlier chapters of this book. The Cambridge Platonists included John Smith (1618-1652) and Peter Sterry (1613-1672). They represented a last spiritual flowering in the universities, which since then have become more and more secular. Thomas Traherne (1637-1674) was another notable English Platonist. After the Platonists, William Law (1686-1761) was perhaps one of England's greatest mystical writers.

We have said earlier, that if one must try to put a date on the end of the Middle Ages, the date of 1312, marking the destruction of the Templars, is significant. It can, in a sense, be taken as indicating the beginning of the end. The end is perhaps marked by 1492, when Ferdinand and Isabella commenced the expulsion of the Muslims from Spain. This was not an ethnic or racist expulsion; people of Moorish descent, Moriscos as they were called, were allowed to stay if they became, or convincingly appeared to become, Christians. Most of them were, however, expelled at a later date. This expulsion of the Muslims marked the final break between East and West, for Islam had functioned as a link between the two. From then on, the West isolated itself intellectually from the rest of the world. It is possible that Islamic esoterism - Sufism - may have persisted secretly for a time in Southern Spain. One of the *fandangos de Huelva - el cante grande,* or the great songs of the flamenco style - begins: *"Tengo tu nombre apuntao, en las murailles de mi corazon,"* meaning "I have thy name written down on the walls of my heart." Although this can be taken literally as a love song, it may also refer to Sufism, the invocation of the name of Majesty of God, *Allah,* on the outside of the heart, implying a return to the primordial state of True Man.

Amongst the writers of post-mediaeval Western Europe, three names stand out: Rabelais, Cervantes, and Shakespeare. All three included a mystical content in their writings, but, like the secret societies and the alchemists, they had to hide their mysticism beneath an exterior which seemed quite different. Rabelais chose bawdy humour, presenting himself to the world as an erudite buffoon; Cervantes used straightforward humour; Shakespeare chose the theatre, using its full range from bawdy comedy to dramatic tragedy.

Rabelais, one of the greatest Renaissance writers, has often been misunderstood by commentators who have looked at his works superficially and labelled him as a humanist and even an athiest. In the prologue to his first book, he implies that one must break its bones and suck the marrow; in other words the profound meanings are well-concealed. Commenting on monasteries, he said that during the Middle Ages the noble families sent the best, and most intelligent of their children into them; whereas in his time, they used them as a dumping ground for imbeciles and problem children, reserving the best of their offspring for worldly pursuits. Rabelais described his ideal community, ideal in the sense of an esoteric alternative to mediaeval monasticism, in a section of his first book, entitled the Abbey of Thélème. This 'abbey' would have no walls around it, and his description of the building is typical of an early sixteenth century Renaissance chateau. There would be no clocks nor other devices for measuring time, and the inhabitants would be men and women who would be free to marry and not bound by the vows and rules typical of monasticism. They would dress in the fashions of the times, could be rich, and do the sort of things done by the inhabitants of any contemporary chateau; hunting, for example. In fact, the only difference would be that early in the morning the women would decide how they were all going to dress that day; and, during the day, if anyone said, for example, "let us drink," they would all drink; likewise if anyone said, "let us play" or "let us go hunting," they would all do so. In other words, the members of the community would seem just like those of any other contemporary chateau, but with one important difference; they would be protected from the mental speculation that goes with fashion, decision-making, and clock watching; this would leave them mentally free to concentrate on some spiritual method whilst seeming just like other people in a comparable station in life. Although Rabelais described his ideal community as an 'abbey,' he was advocating an active spiritual life, what the Hindus call karma yoga, and not one of cloistered retreat. He was therefore concerned not so much with harping back to the Middle Ages as with adapting to the conditions of the Renaissance, making use of its advantages, whilst avoiding the spiritual disadvantages of speculative worldliness. He clearly regarded secrecy as of great importance, affording the protection that was once provided by surrounding monastic walls. He recommended much of the learning of the Renaissance, but warned against subjects such as divinatory astrology and certain writings on alchemy, which he said were an abuse and a vanity. He also commented on the foolishness of prayer as personal petition, pointing out that asking for money, for example, could be asking too much (for money given to one has to be taken away from another). If one must ask for something in prayer, he added, one should ask for health, since that may be granted without taking anything away from others.

Cervantes was born in Spain in 1547. In 1575 he was captured by pirates and taken to Algiers where he became the slave of a renegade Greek. His friends and family took a long time in collecting his ransom, so he tried to escape on three occasions, each time without success. He was finally ransomed in 1580. Whether he had any contact with the esoteric side of Islam during his captivity will probably remain unknown, for the final expulsion of the Moriscos, by Philip the Third, had taken place, and his writings could not safely have hinted at anything of the kind. His greatest work, Don Quixote, was published in two parts, in 1604 and 1614. In it, he included an account of a captive's life in the Islamic world which showed the captors in a fairly bad light.

Don Quixote is an amusing story of the adventures of a man who insisted on becoming a knight-errant too late, in the sixteenth century. Cervantes wrote the story as an antidote to the then current preoccupation with popular ballads and romances of chivalry, which had lost the symbolism of knighthood as an initiatic way, and were verging on sheer fantasy. He used this humorous story, however, to include many things serious, and also to show that the literal way of the knight was no longer practicable as a spiritually-operative way. He included a comment in the story, that King Arthur was flying about Britain in the form of a raven*. He also included a meeting with a Green Man, who turned up just before Don Quixote was about to have a dangerous encounter with some lions. The lions became docile and not interested in fighting, perhaps through the invisible effect of the Green Man's presence. Don Quixote spent a few days at the Green Man's house, where he was impressed by the marvellous silence through the whole house, "which seemed like a Carthusian monastery." The dialogue in the book, between the Green Man and Don Quixote, is, of course, Cervante's and not to be imputed to the former in any literal way. At the end of the book, although Cervantes had ridiculed the idea of

*There is a similar story relating to Castell Dinas Bran, a castle near Llangollen in North Wales. It is said that in the old days, a talking raven used to warn the Keeper of the Castle whenever hostile forces were approaching.

21. Castell Dinas Bran
(after an old copper engraving).

138

**22. Don Quixote, his 'squire' Sancho Panza,
and others**
(after Vanderbank copper engraving).

following a way of knighthood in his times, he nonetheless let his hero succeed in the conquest of death, giving him the following epitaph:

"Here lies the gentle knight and stout
Who to such height of valour got
That if you mark his deeds throughout,
Death over his life triumphed not
With bringing of his death about.

The world as nothing did he prize,
For as a scarecrow in man's eyes
He lived, and was their bugbear too;
And had the luck, with much ado,
To live a fool, and yet die wise."

The letters 'IXO' in Quixote can be brought together, with the 'X' horizontal, forming a three-dimensional cross in a circle, or sphere, symbolising the world-centre, in the spiritual sense.

Cervantes died in 1615, only a year after the completion of his great work.

Shakespeare crystallised and fixed the initiatic and profound wisdom of the Middle Ages, hiding it in his plays where it would remain for future generations to discover. The key to understanding Shakespeare is to look at his works not with the eyes of modern man, but from the point of view of the ancient and traditional worlds. We have already quoted Shakespeare's reference to the present era as 'this iron age.' Regarding the upside-down sense of values of these late times, he writes:

"For in the fatness of these pursey times,
Virtue itself of vice must pardon beg*."

His view of destiny is implied in:

"There's a divinity which shapes our ends,
Rough hew them as we will*.".

His view of the purpose of life, and the world, is summarized in his famous passage: "All the world's a stage, and all the men and women merely players."

*Hamlet III, iv.

This traditional view of life stands in sharp contrast to the modern one of seeing individual life as the pursuit of material wealth and pleasure, and the world as a place subject to progressive improvement. Modern man's emphasis is on doing, with the intention of materially improving himself, and sometimes also the world around him. Shakespeare's is one of being and becoming, hence Hamlet's famous phrase "to be, or not to be." The idea of people as actors on the stage of life is closer to the old idea of fulfilling a function in life, rather than cultivating the individuality; likewise the emphasis on being rather than doing is related to man's becoming in a spiritual sense. In this analogy of a stage, modern man often imagines he is the playwright as well as, or instead of, the actor, hence much of the conflict of our times.

Echoing the Delphic inscription "know thyself," Shakespeare says of one of his characters that he is "one that, above all other strifes, contended especially to know himself*." His advice to one who would begin the spiritual life by the cultivation of virtue and abstinence from sin, goes:

"Assume a virtue, if you have it not.
That monster, custom, who all sense doth eat,
That to the use of actions fair and good,
He likewise gives a frock or livery,
That aptly is put on. Refrain to-night;
And that shall lend a kind of easiness
To the next abstinence: the next more easy;
For use almost can change the stamp of nature,
And master ev'n the devil or throw him out
With wondrous potency**."

Shakespeare's notion of spiritual death and rebirth is made clear in:

"To sue to live, I find I seek to die,
And, seeking death, find life***."

Whatever were the real merits of the historical Henry

*Measure for Measure III, ii.
**Hamlet III, iv.
***Measure for Measure III, i.

the Fifth, Shakespeare chose him to represent twice-born man, one who is fit to reign as True King over himself and others. In Henry IV, the young Prince Hal spends his time 'living it up' in apparently dubious company in the Thames-side taverns of London. Whilst his father worries about this behaviour of his heir, Warwick tells him:

> "The prince will in the perfection of time
> Cast off his followers; and their memory
> Shall as a pattern or a measure live
> By which his Grace must mete the lives of others,
> Turning past evils to advantages*."

The casting off of his followers may be interpreted literally, as casting off bad company; more profoundly, it can be seen as a casting off of the multiple parts of his own ego or self, at a time of spiritual death and rebirth. Apart from the question of coming to know his own self, and to hate it - which is a necessary condition of the mystical way - the young prince, by larking about in the taverns, obtains first-hand experience of the people he will later govern; experience which will enable him to govern with greater understanding. When the old king is dead, and the prince is on his way to be crowned Henry V, he says to Falstaff:

> "I know thee not, old man...
> Presume not that I am the thing I was;
> For God doth know, so shall the world perceive,
> That I have turned away my former self;
> So will I those that kept me company**."

The words "presume not that I am the thing I was" can

*Henry IV part 2. IV, iv. In this context, Lao Zi, or Lao Tzu, wrote: "The Sages have said that he who rejects neither moral filth nor political evil is capable of becoming the chief of a territory, or sovereign of the empire. These words are quite true, though they offend many." The meaning, within the context of Lao Zi's book, is that although a ruler should have cast off the filth and evil of his own self, he should have experienced the ways of the world so that he may be supple enough to accommodate himself to it, and not be a rigid and systematic person; he should temper justice with mercy through experience.
**Henry IV part 2. V, v.

be taken as referring to the death of the prince's former self, and his rebirth as a New Man; a True King. This part of Shakespeare's play also contains the theme of 'the king must die,' for Henry IV must die before Prince Hal can be reborn. In this part of the play, Henry IV can be regarded as symbolising Prince Hal's self, the Old Man that must die for him to be reborn as a New Man.

Some have seen Falstaff as an attractive character, a likeable rogue; others have seen him, on analysis, as wickedness itself. Shakespeare certainly let some of his characters see Falstaff in a bad light. If, however, he was so wicked, Shakespeare would surely have damned him. We find, however, at the beginning of Henry V, that Falstaff has died mentioning the name of God. Those who are familiar with Hamlet may recall that the latter withdrew from killing his enemy when he found him at prayer, for, in Shakespeare's eyes, to die in prayer would save his soul. Perhaps Shakespeare envisaged Falstaff as a dual-purpose character; one on the lines of Rabelais who outwardly acted the bawdy buffoon, but who was quite different inside. Prince Hal's rejection of Falstaff can then be seen as an attempt to protect him from political reprisals, for many at court feared Falstaff's influence on the new king. There is, of course, no doubt that the prince is at the same time rejecting his former way of life, and company. There can be little doubt also that Falstaff's exterior symbolises part of Prince Hal's inferior self, to which he has died a spiritual death. Shakespeare seems to have used Falstaff, the seeming buffoon, to put forward views which would be unpopular with many of his audience if they were put in the mouth of a serious character. We are thinking here especially of Falstaff's derisory speech: "Honour, what is honour?" Shakespeare no doubt recognised honour as a noble sentiment, but the upper classes of his day had made it paramount, whereas, for Shakespeare, there were other, spiritual values which should rank highest. Shakespeare also used Falstaff to voice an idea of reincarnation:

> "Do you not remember, 'a saw a flea stick upon Bardolph's nose, and 'a said it was a black soul burning in hell fire*."

*Henry V. II, iii.

In Othello, Shakespeare had no difficulty in portraying Iago as wickedness itself; a devil incarnate. He could perhaps have done likewise for Falstaff; that he did not do so, may imply that he intended him to have an exterior that belied his interior*.

Readers are referred to Martin Ling's book, 'The Secret of Shakespeare,' for a more detailed discussion of the mystical nature of his works, especially those of the last fifteen years of his life.

If the passage from the Middle Ages to the Renaissance was marked by a general change from spirituality to worldliness, that which marked the Industrial Revolution and the entrance into modern times saw a channelling of worldliness into materialism, with all things non-material kept more for sentimental, than intellectual reasons. None of these changes should, however, be seen as things which should not have happend, no more than one should say that a flower should not lose its petals, or winter not follow autumn. The flower is followed by the fruit, winter by a new spring. Each succeeding period has its deficits, but also its compensations. The Middle Ages, as we have already pointed out, were far from perfect, despite their spiritual advantages. The Renaissance and Post-Renaissance periods were characterized by worldliness, but there were the craft initiations, secret societies, and 'new' ways represented by the revival of interest in alchemy and Platonism. With the Industrial Revolution, most of the craft initiatic societies were destroyed or denatured, and those other secret societies that had not already folded up, just faded away. Although this represents a loss, modern times have the compensation that much of the older initiatic knowledge which had been kept secret, is now generally available in books to those who seek it; sacred writings of East and West, once only available to the few, are nowadays accessible to all. The biggest dangers of the present times, are of materialism breaking down into pure fantasy in popular cults of escapism, and through the abuse of drugs. The would-be seeker in modern times also runs the risk of being deceived by the plethora of false spiritual ways offered by false Masters, and organisations falsely claiming descent from the old initiatic and

*The name Falstaff may be interpreted in two ways: False-Staff, and Fal-Staff.

secret societies, and even using their names.

The signs of the times - whether one looks at the traditional prophesies, or at some of the modern prophets of doom - seem ominous. The modern prophets of doom point to the dangers of world population increase, exhaustion of natural resources, environmental deterioration and destruction, nuclear disaster, germ and chemical warfare, often in a context which seems hopeless. The Christian and Islamic prophesies speak of the coming of Antichrist and a period of great destruction, before the second coming of Christ. The Buddhists are awaiting the coming of the Maitraya Buddha; the Hindus the Kalki Avatara. The latter is described as seated on a white horse with a rod in his hand and a sword in his mouth; this description so resembles that of the second coming of Christ, that it is reasonable to believe that one and the same person is implied in the prophesies of the different traditions*.

Whilst the modern prophets of doom predict either total annihilation, or a few survivors living in a new Dark Age of hardship and gloom, the traditional prophesies see the possibility of a new humanity in a new Golden Age, like the phoenix rising from its ashes, like a new spring following a hard destructive winter. The traditional view can be likened to an idea of Divine Alchemy in which this base humanity is subjected to drastic measures which eliminate the baseness and transform what is left into 'gold.'

But what of the period between now and that phase of destruction? The Ramayana, the great Hindu epic which purports to come from the age before the present one, speaks of a blessed period at the end of the Age of Kali (the Iron Age) when all acts will be futile and mantra-yoga will reign supreme**. The Islamic tradition similarly promises a spiritual revival before the end; in this respect, the Koran adds: "And we have never destroyed a nation without first sending a warner." Black Elk, a spiritual chief of the Sioux Indians, had a vision in the 1870's

---

*"And there shall be one fold, and one shepherd," John X, 15. Note that this should not be interpreted in any ecumenical sense of bringing existing world religions together; it should be seen as a return to the Primordial Tradition for the next cycle of humanity, if there is to be one.
**As with Shakespeare, the emphasis is on being, through mantra, rather than on acting or doing.

in which he saw the sacred hoop (or circle) of the nation broken, and the people leave the good red road for the black road of every man for himself; at the end of his vision he saw these things restored, implying perhaps a similar spiritual redress before the end of this age of humanity.

For there to be any spiritual awakening before the end of this cycle of human history, people would have to become quite fed-up with themselves and the world they live in, for most people cannot begin holy warfare without first seeing the evil of their own selves*, and the illusory nature of their own world. The Chinese Sage** said: "Perfect peace cannot reign in this world until people seek the cause of their own ills in their own interior imperfection." The rod of iron of the Second Coming may be interpreted as people having to be driven*** on the spiritual way; the sword in the mouth as words of truth which will be piercing or cutting because the truth will come as a shock. This may imply that something of a fairly drastic nature may occur before any period of spiritual change, perhaps like a dress rehersal for the opening night of the final showdown. In an earlier chapter we pointed out that Dante's experience at the centre of Hell was one of total inversion; he had to put his head where his feet were to get out of that state and begin the ascent towards Heaven. From a spiritual point of view, this humanity is heading towards an inversion of the traditional values, and individuals towards an inversion of the values symbolised by the army hierarchy of heart (spirit) - mind - body - sex. When things are upside-down, they can be put right more quickly than when they are mixed-up, just by turning the whole thing over. This hints at the spiritual possibilities of the last times, and helps to explain why the

*There is an old saying: "You can't make a saint out of a choir boy." The reason for this is that those who see themselves as pure and good cannot improve because they see no need for it. Only those who see the evil of their own selves, can begin to change.
**Zhuang Zi (Chuang Tsu).
***This should not be interpreted as people being forced by religious fanatics; it should be understood more in the sense of the forces of karma, or destiny, driving them along. In Islam, Christ is reported as saying that when he is in front, all is well, but if he is behind, he is terrible.

Hindu Tradition refers to them as blessed. It should go without saying, however, that to become aware of the foregoing and deliberately pursue a pesonal policy of completing the inversion, or even one of not resisting temptation, would most certainly be self-destructive; it could lead to insanity, and would not result in spiritual improvement.

This question of topsy-turviness occurs in the prophesy of Merlin: "Men will turn their backs on heaven, and fix their eyes on earth..." and "roots and branches shall change their places..." This may be taken as referring to a time when people's senses of values will be upside-down, and when people themselves will show signs of inversion. The same may also refer to the inversion of traditional symbols (and therefore their misinterpretation); this is said to be one of the signs of the coming of Antichrist. Apart from the inversion of vertical symbols such as the Tree of Life, there are modern examples of rotational symbols which have been made to rotate in the opposite way to their traditional representation. There is no doubt that phallic symbolism played a role in many traditions, past and present, associated amongst other things with fertility and world-renewal rites. But to assume, as many moderns have, that any traditional symbol which points upwards is phallic, is to misinterpret those which in reality represent the idea of the spiritual pole, or world axis, best known from the Tree of Life. The above-mentioned prophesy of Merlin, in Geoffrey of Monmouth's 'History,' includes also a reference to the Cornish Oak flourishing, and the land of Cambria (Wales) being filled with joy; perhaps we can see here a reference to a possibility of a spiritual change in the West towards the end of this cycle of history. According to the Glastonbury legends, the tomb of Joseph of Arimathea will be rediscovered, perhaps as a 'sign,' before the end. One wonders whether the Chalice Well at Glastonbury holds a secret in this connection.

A Christian prophesy of inversion can be seen in the Book of Ecclesiastes, which says: "I have seen servants upon horses, and princes* walking as servants upon the earth." An expanded Christian view of these later times is

*Ecclesiastes X, 7. We remind readers that in this context 'prince' refers to one who has the qualities of a True Prince, and not one who bears the title without the qualities.

to be seen in the Second Epistle to Timothy:

"This know also, that in the last days perilous times shall come. For men shall be lovers of their own selves, covetous, boasters, proud, blasphemers, disobedient to parents, unthankful, unholy. Without natural affection, truce breakers, false accusors, incontinent, fierce, despisers of those that are good. Traitors, heady, highminded, lovers of pleasures more than lovers of God... Ever learning, and never able to come to the knowledge of the truth*."

The last comment is particularly apt for modern times, for never has man had so much learning, in the sense of information, and yet so little wisdom.

In Islam, three of the signs of the coming of Antichrist are: Tall buildings everywhere, women going half-naked, and inferior persons leading nations. There is also a saying that when one sees these signs of the times, one should turn to the first part of the Surah, or Chapter, of the Cave, in the Koran. The latter includes a reference to sleepers in a cave. Some Western commentators have interpreted this part as a reference to the Seven Sleepers of Ephesus, who did a Rip-Van-Winkle to survive a period which was hostile to Christianity. Although some may argue that the Koran may not refer to these early Christians, the same surah contains another reference which has been linked with Alexander the Great, also a non-Muslim in the historical sense. One is left wondering if this reference to sleepers in a cave has anything to do with the Celtic legends - of Finn Mac Cumhal and his companions, of Arthur and his knights, and also of Owain Glyndwr - who are said to be sleeping in caves to return to humanity at the appointed time, when they will bring about some form of redress.

These legends of sleepers in a cave can be interpreted literally, or they can be taken as implying the return to humanity of the spiritual and other qualities represented by those people. There are, however, other traditions implying that people will come back from the past to restore knowledge which has been lost.

Another Islamic sign of the last times, is of the sun's

*Timothy III, 1 et seq.

rising in the West. This can be interpreted metaphorically as a spiritual restoration in the West, either the Maghreb (the West of the Islamic world) or the West in general; it can also be interpreted literally, possibly in association with a change in the earth's polarity, something which is recognised as happening from time to time by modern geophysicists. Another Islamic sign of those times is that the moon shall be red and the sun shall be blue; what is remarkable about this is that the Plains Indians of North America have, since late last century, been praying for the coming of the 'sacred red and blue days!'

If we return now to our earlier comment, with reference to Dante's inversion at the centre of Hell, and the spiritual possibilities of correcting the inversion towards the end of this cycle, we can add other ways of looking at the same idea of spiritual advantage towards the end of time. The best known is perhaps Christ's parable of the workers in the vineyard. In that story, those who worked only for a short time, late in the day, received the same wages as those who had worked all day. Although this can be interpreted as relating to Christianity in the context of long-term world history, it may also be taken as relating to the reward for spiritual practice made in the last days of this humanity, at a time when few feel inclined to do so. In Islam, there is a saying of the Prophet Muhammad: "In the last times, he who accomplishes one tenth of what is now prescribed, will be saved." In the latter saying the word accomplish is important, for rites performed when the mind is wandering or distracted, are not accomplished. Regarding the difficulties of living in the last times, a chapter of the Koran called The Declining Day - *Surat Al Asr* - speaks of those who endure with patience. This question of patience is of great importance to modern seekers, in view of the anti-spiritual nature of modern times, and also because of the danger of being tempted into a false spiritual way. Those who think they cannot find a way should remember that the beginning is to ask, through prayer, within oneself, and to be patient, which is difficult; so much so that there is a somewhat exaggerated saying: 'Patience is a virtue found seldom in a woman, and never in a man.'

Another important point for life in modern times is to remember Christ's words 'judge not lest ye be judged yourself.' The reason for stressing this is that in the old days heroes could often be distinguished from villains by their actions; whereas in modern times one can seldom tell the true interior natures of people from what they are doing; many who are inwardly not too bad have been deceived, tricked, or forced by circumstances into occupations or practices which are far from good, others who seem dedicated to doing good may sometimes be inwardly evil in their motives; sheep in wolves' clothing and wolves in sheeps' clothing. Some people, of course, are still what they seem, but the times are so mixed-up that one cannot always tell the sheep from the wolves. It is also important to consider that if there is eventually any spiritual change, it will probably be outwardly almost imperceptible; it will certainly have nothing in common with any modern fundamental or political movements of any shade or colour. Fundamental movements are generally preoccupied with criticism, and with a desire for revenge and justice, a justice which is not tempered by mercy. Whilst there are no doubt many things to criticise in the world, a preoccupation with criticism can become an obsession which is anti-spiritual. Furthermore, criticism, even when justified, can attract so many enemies that any spiritual possibilities one may have, will be jeopardised because, to put it in its mildest form, having many enemies means having no peace. Any period of change before the end is likely to be brief, only a few years; long enough to give people a chance to have some interior spiritual development, but too short for any major social or legislative changes; but one can expect changes resulting from people becoming more virtuous.

Having written about prophesies, we think it right to add a word of warning not to become preoccupied with them, for it can lead to an obsession which can be quite anti-spiritual. Repetition of prophesies of disaster and doom can only help to bring the latter about. Repetition of any kind of prophesy can also attract enemies to oneself. We have only included the foregoing paragraphs with some hesitation, and because there is a need to show that there is some hope left, despite the modern prophets of gloom and despair. A preoccupation with the future can also be anti-spiritual because it prevents one from having any possibility of realising the eternal present.

In the modern West there is a great deal of interest in survival. Many, especially in the United States, are arming and training themselves for survival in some period when they expect law and order to break down; others, in the United States and elsewhere, are constructing private bunkers with stocks of provisions, in which to survive a nuclear holocaust. None of these things guarantee survival. Those who seek to survive by force of arms may well fall victim to other, similar groups who fear them because they are armed; those who seek to avoid radiation may fall to the effects of germ warfare; those who store up provisions may fall to others who wish to steal what they have. In saying this, we are not implying that one should not be prepared for difficult times, but simply pointing out that certain types of preparation do not guarantee survival. When Rome was finally sacked, the poor people in the catacombs went hungry, but they were not touched because they had nothing worth stealing; those who perished were the rich who had planned to survive and barricaded themselves in their houses with arms, valuables, and provisions. In this context, we add a very relevant quote from Zhuang Zi, the Chinese Sage:

"When Zhuang Zi was crossing the mountains, he saw a great tree with long and luxuriant branches. A woodman who was cutting wood nearby did not touch this tree.
'Why not?' asked Zhuang Zi.
'Because its wood is good-for-nothing,' said the woodman.
'The fact of being good-for-nothing is valuable to this tree, allowing it to live until its natural death,' concluded Zhuang Zi.
After crossing the mountains, Zhuang Zi received hospitality at a friend's house. Happy to see him again, the master of the house told his servant to kill a duck and cook it.
'Which of our two ducks should I kill?' asked the servant, 'the one that quacks, or the mute one?'
'The mute one,' said the master.
The next day the disciple who accompanied Zhuang Zi said to him: 'Yesterday the tree was saved because it was good-for-nothing; the duck was killed because it could not quack; therefore, being capable or incapable, which one saves?'
'That depends on the case,' said Zhuang Zi laughing.

'One single thing saves in all cases; it is to be elevated to the knowledge of the Principle and its action, and to keep oneself in indifference and abstraction. Such a man thinks as little of praise as of blame. He knows how to rise up like the dragon, and to flatten himself like the serpent, bending himself to circumstances. He frolics in the bosom of the ancestor of all things (the Principle)... Come what may, he fears nothing.'"

The Arthurian quest is still highly relevant to modern times, provided it is not taken literally, but in its intention. The knights of old lived an interior spiritual life; their exterior function was the repression of evil, whenever and wherever they came face-to-face with it. As far back as the sixteenth century, Cervantes pointed out that it was impracticable to literally imitate the way of the knight. In modern times, we add that it is impracticable to imitate even the exterior function of the knight, the suppression of the evil around us, at least without first having overcome the evil within our own selves. The modern world is full of sincere crusaders who are actively involved in opposing things, groups, or organisations - political or otherwise - which they see as evil. Sometimes they are wrong, sometimes they are right in what they see as evil; but even in the latter case they seldom succeed, and are often duped by self-seekers who make good use of their sincerity for their own ends. This is what the Ramayana means when it describes acts as futile at the end of the Iron Age. Despite this, an active way is clearly recommended for these times; it is simply a question of confining one's acts to virtuous ones, and not acting like those who wish to change the world from without, and whose actions often merely replace one set of evils with another.

From a spiritual point of view, such people are putting the cart before the horse; imitating the external way of the knight, without the internal spiritual way; trying to change the world without making the least effort to change their own interior. The way of the knight is part of what the Hindus call karma-yoga, the yoga of action, destiny, and vocation. The 'secret' of the initiatic orders of knighthood is none other than that of a spiritual life hidden behind activity in the world. There is nothing weird or magical about this secret, except the 'magic' of the death of the self and rebirth to a spiritual life. This is not meant to imply that there was no other secret knowledge in ancient times; even applied knowledge, such as medicine, was often kept secret to prevent unscrupulous people from misusing it. There is no doubt that a great deal of ancient knowledge has been lost, often because its custodians failed to find anyone of suitable calibre to whom they could hand it down. The knights of old may have had secret and powerful prayers similar to the secret mantras one reads about in the Hindu epics, but these were, in a sense, accessories, and their real secret was none other than the general initiatic secret, hiding their spiritual life behind a mask of outward activity. Although the Templars may have been the natural heritors of a tradition of knighthood coming down from the time of King Arthur, or before, we do not see in this the need to claim there was a completely separate and 'secret tradition' which has been passed from secret organisation to another. Those who have claimed there was such a 'secret tradition' have perhaps failed to recognise that traditional initiatic organisations all have certain things in common, but these common elements are not necessarily evidence of direct links, or 'borrowings.' What made King Arthur's initiatic order of knighthood great, was perhaps not so much a question of a body of secret knowledge, as that it had, in the person of Arthur, a truly great leader and Spiritual Master.

The second coming of King Arthur, if it should ever happen in a literal sense, need not be interpreted politically. It should be seen more as his return as 'pole' or Spiritual Master, rather than as a temporal king. When King Herod heard of the birth of Jesus, one 'born to be king,' he likewise misinterpreted the phrase to imply a king in the temporal sense.

The literal vocation of the knight no longer exists, but people have their own active way of life which brings them into contact with others. In modern times, the functional equivalent of the exterior life of the knight should be the practice of virtue; the fight against evil should be an internal one; an internal struggle that leads towards spiritual perfection and real freedom; the only quest which is truly worth-while, for the individual, and the world.

153

REFERENCES AND FURTHER READING.

(Note, for a more comprehensive list of references to the mystical way, see the book by Whitall N. Perry; likewise, for the Arthurian literature see the books by Richard Cavendish, and N. J. Lacy.)

Adhamnan, St. see the book by C. S. Boswell.
Anderson, William. **Dante the Maker.**
                         Routledge and Kegan Paul, 1980.
Apuleius. See the book by Head and Cranston.
Black Elk. See the book by Neihardt, J. G.
Bhagavad Gita. There are several translations, including one by Swami Paramananda in **The Wisdom of China and India,** edited by Lin Yutang, Random House. N. Y. 1942; one by Shri Purohit Swami, Faber and Faber, 1978; and
                         one by Juan Mascaro, Penguin Books, 1962.
Boswell, C. S. **An Irish Precursor of Dante.** London. 1908.
Bulfinch, T. **The Age of Chivalry and the Legends of Charlemagne.** Mentor, N.Y. 1962 (reprint of 1858/62).
Cavendish, Richard. **King Arthur and the Grail.**
                         Paladin, 1980.
Cervantes, Miguel de, **Don Quixote.** Penguin Books, 1950.
Coomaraswamy, Ananda. **Hinduism and Buddhism.**
                         New York Philosophical Library, 1943.
Darqawi, Shaikh. **Letters of a Sufi Master.**
     Trans. Titus Burkhardt. Perennial Books, London, 1969.
Eckhart, **Master Eckhart.** Trans. C. de B. Evans.
                         John M. Watkins, London, 1924.
Geoffrey of Monmouth. **History of the Kings of Britain.**
                         Penguin Books.
Glory of the world, the (or **The Table of Paradise**).
     Anonymous alchemical treatise forming part of the
                         Hermetic Museum, in Latin, Frankfort, 1678.
                         John M. Watkins, London, 1953.
                         (reprint of first English edition of 1893).
Goullert, Peter. **The Monastery of the Jade Mountain.**
                         John Murray, London. 1961.
Head, Joseph, and Cranston, S. L., **Reincarnation, an East-West anthology.** Julian Press, N.Y. 1961.
Hermes (Trismegistus), **Hermetica.** Trans. Walter Scott.
                         4 vols. Oxford, Clarendon Press. 1924-36.
Ibn 'Arabi, **Sufis of Andalusia.** Trans. R. W. J. Austin.
     Univ. of California Press, Berkley, Los Angeles, 1971.

Koran, the Meaning of the Glorious.
Trans. Mohammed Marmaduke Picthall, Mentor.

Lacy, N. J. (ed.) **The Arthurian Encyclopedia.**
garland Press, N.Y. 1986.

Lambspring, Abraham. **The Book of Lambspring.**
Hermetic Museum. Vol 1. John M. Watkins, London, 1953.

Law, William. Quoted from the book by Whitall Perry.

Le Braz, Anatole. **Celtic Legend of the Beyond.**
Trans. D Bryce. Llanerch, 1986.

Lings, M. **The Secret of Shakespeare.**
Aguarian Press, 1984.

Luzel, F. M. **Celtic Folk-Tales from Armorica.**
Trans. D Bryce. Llanerch. 1985.

Manava Dharma Shastra. The Ordinances of Manu.
Trans. Arthur Coke Burnell. London. Trubner. 1884.

Matgioi, **La Voie Metaphysique.**
Les Editions Traditionnelles, Paris. 1936.

Milarepa, the Life of. Adapted from the original translation of W Evans-Wentz by Lobzang Jivaka.
John Murray. 1962.

Minzing, Abbot. See the book by P. Goullert.

Neihardt, J. G. **Black Elk Speaks.** Abacus. 1974.

Nicholas of Cusa. **Of Learned Ignorance.**
Trans. Fr. Germaine Heron. Routledge & Kegan Paul.

Nizami, **Layla and Majnun.** Luzac & Co., London.

Palacios, Asin. See the book by William Anderson.

Pallis, M. **The Way and the Mountain.** Peter Owen. 1960.

Perry, Whitall N. **A Treasury of Traditional Wisdom.**
George Allen and Unwin, London. 1971.

Pius XI. Quoted from the book by Marco Pallis (p.68).

Rabelais. **Gargantua and Pantagruel.**
Samuel Putnam version. Viking Press. 1946.

Rolleston, T. W. **Myths and Legends of the Celtic Race.**
Constable, London, 1985.

Sir Gawain and the Green Knight.*
Prose version by W R J Barron.
Manchester University Press. 1974.

The Sophic Hydrolyth (or, **Water Stone of the Wise).**
Anonymous. Part of the **Hermetic Museum.**
John M. Watkins, London. 1953.

The Tibetan Book of the Dead. Trans. Frank J. MacHovec.
Peter Pauper Press, N.Y. 1972.

Valentine, Basil. **Practica. Hermetic Museum,** vol 1.
John M. Watkins, London. 1953.

Way of a Pilgrim, the. Anonymous Russian work.

Society for the Promotion of Christian Knowledge.

Wieger, L. **Wisdom of the Daoist Masters.**

The works of Lao Zi, Lie Zi, and Zhuang Zi.

Trans. Derek Bryce. Llanerch. 1984.

Wu Ch'eng-en. **Monkey.** Trans. Arthur Waley.

Penguin Books.

*Note: Sir Gawain and the Green Knight. There is also a translation in modern English Poetry, by B. Stone (Penguin Books), and a version in Middle-English by J. R. R. Tolkien and E. V. Gordon (Clarendon Press, Oxford).

INDEX

Books by the same author:

EVOLUTION AND THE NEW PHYLOGENY.

A review of the controversy over the **punctuated equilibria** pattern in the fossil record. A useful updating book for lecturers, teachers, and undergraduates; it can also be read by intelligent sixth-formers taking biology.

ISBN 0947992057

GRASSLAND SMALLHOLDING.

Written with co-author Dr. Arabella Wagenaar. A guide to small and medium acreage pastoral farming. Aimed at the beginner, this realistic, practical book can also be of value to those already engaged in smallholding because of its illustrated d.-i.-y. content.

ISBN 0947992030

Published by Llanerch Enterprises.
Printed by Cambrian News, Aberystwyth.